NIETZSCHE'S RECLAMATION OF PHILOSOPHY

D1483660

VIBS

Volume 54

Robert Ginsberg
Executive Editor

Associate Editors

G. John M. Abbarno
Virginia Black
H. G. Callaway
Rem B. Edwards
Rob Fisher
Dane R. Gordon
Heta Häyry
Matti Häyry
Richard T. Hull
Joseph C. Kunkel
Ruth M. Lucier
Alan Milchman
George David Miller
Michael H. Mitias
Samuel M. Natale
Peter A. Redpath
Alan Rosenberg
Arleen Salles
Daniel Statman

a volume in
Central-European Value Studies
CEVS
H. G. Callaway, Editor

NIETZSCHE'S RECLAMATION OF PHILOSOPHY

Kathleen J. Wininger

Amsterdam - Atlanta, GA 1997

Cover design by Chris Kok based on a photograph, ©1984 by Robert Ginsberg, of statuary by Gustav Vigeland in the Frogner Park, Oslo, Norway.

∞ The paper on which this book is printed meets the requirements of "ISO 9706:1994, Information and documentation - Paper for documents - Requirements for permanence".

ISBN: 90-420-0383-9
©Editions Rodopi B.V., Amsterdam - Atlanta, GA 1997
Printed in The Netherlands

3
677YWi
997

For Florence Witt Shomer

CONTENTS

EDITORIAL FOREWORD

In her book, *Nietzsche's Reclamation of Philosophy*, Kathleen J. Wininger speaks of the new meaning which Nietzsche gave to philosophy, and she seeks to reclaim Nietzsche as philosopher. Following Wininger, Nietzsche's philosophy is not the academic concern with arguments and canonical texts; instead, Nietzsche's philosophy is hermeneutic and interpretive. It is a philosophy oriented to lived experience and to the exploration of values which go to constitute lived experience. Nietzsche's approach was to understand texts on the basis of their own historical and cultural context, seeking out matters of vital importance. The aim is the transformation of our own culture and our own values.

Wininger stresses Nietzsche's rejection of the myths of "pure reason" and "absolute knowledge." Our interpretive powers depend on making good use of our own perspectives. We require an experimental eye which sees, in its various ways, through our engagement with values. This hermeneutic seeing refuses to blind itself through feigned neutrality. Wininger understands Nietzsche as a precursor and practitioner of hermeneutic methods, and there are suggestions too of Nietzsche as precursor of what Hans Joas has called "the hidden pragmatism of Max Scheler and Martin Heidegger."

Wininger aims to refute Nietzsche's genuine excesses, in Nietzschean style, by ignoring them and concentrating on the genuine value of Nietzsche's work. Yet she urges that much of what is regarded as excessive requires finer interpretation. Thus, she is concerned to evaluate interpretations of Nietzsche arising from Walter Kaufmann and Arthur Danto, as well as interpretive points from Cornel West, Michel Foucault, and Jacques Derrida. Part of what is recommended is a Nietzschean genealogy of contemporary social issues such as racism and the subjugation of women.

Throughout the book there is a sustained focus on moral and aesthetic values and on Nietzsche's genealogical method. In her approach to Nietzsche, Wininger shows many European influences, and she is concerned to bring these influences to bear both on American conceptions of philosophy and on contemporary social problems.

This book is the second volume of the Central-European Value Studies (CEVS), a special series of the Value Inquiry Book Series (VIBS). CEVS is a pluralistic project which publishes books in all areas of value inquiry originating from Central Europe, its major philosophical traditions, and the German-speaking world in particular. The purpose of the special series is to make Central-European studies more broadly available in the English-speaking world.

CEVS draws on the talents of a distinguished European Board of Assistant Editors. It is co-sponsored by the Philosophy Seminar of the University of Mainz, Germany, the Centre for Cultural Research of Aarhus University,

Denmark, and the International Academy for Philosophy of the Principality of Liechtenstein.

CEVS aims to help bridge the gap between German-language philosophy and that of the English-speaking world. As Kathleen J. Wininger shows us in the present volume, this bridging requires close attention to tendencies of thought existing on the opposite side of the gap: it essentially involves intercultural dialogue.

H.G. Callaway
Editor, CEVS
Associate Editor, VIBS

AUTHOR'S PREFACE

Friedrich Nietzsche does not have the "proper" attitude toward the important philosophers of the past. He calls Socrates a pleb, and a buffoon who got himself taken seriously. Plato is a monster of pride who saw philosophy as merely erotic contest. Kant is that most deformed conceptual cripple who confused the task of the civil servant with that of the philosopher. Nietzsche makes these criticisms because he wants to emphasize the extent of his distance from the philosophers who preceded him. For him, philosophy always comes from interested inquiry. He enjoys unmasking the interest in the great philosophers who prided themselves on their disinterest, otherworldliness, and objectivity. When we allow ourselves some irreverence; the humor and, dare we say it, the truth of these comments comes to the fore. These are not the last words on Kant, Plato, or Socrates, not even for Nietzsche. They do, however, capture something we as philosophers are trained to ignore; the personality, the motivation and the cultural situation of the thinkers of the past. We can explain away or ignore Nietzsche's comments. But if we do not erase them, they can remind us of some of his goals. He wants to revitalize philosophy. The task is in part an aesthetic one, because he recognizes the power of controlling metaphors. The task is psychological in its attention to unmasking hidden motivations. If he is to engage in hyperbolic attacks on Kant, he cannot spare himself. Nietzsche demands a kind of honesty that is really quite new to much European philosophy.

After reading remarks like the ones mentioned above, we do not expect Nietzsche to have had an easy reception in all intellectual communities. Yet, interest in Nietzsche has grown steadily in the past two decades. Much of this attention has begun to focus on his critiques and style. Thus contemporary work extends early criticism of Nietzsche which labeled him a romantic or an aesthete, an intellectual who was not worthy of serious philosophical interest. Work that has taken Nietzsche seriously as a philosopher, has often done so at the expense of his stylistic talents and the importance of aesthetics in his work. Nietzsche is more than just an elegant and creative writer. His project was more than self creation. To stop at these aspects of his work is to ignore his oft repeated hope for posthumous recognition. He hoped that interpreters would eventually recognize the extent of his critiques, the perspicacity of his observations, and then apply his insights in the construction of new cultural practices.

Nietzsche has a new model of what it is to be a philosopher. This is his positive contribution. In his attempt to revitalize philosophy, he is not so naive as to think he needs to create entirely new ideas of philosophy. As a philologist Nietzsche has a sense of modesty with respect to cultural history. He uses the past in a positive sense and reclaims some of its strategies. A great many diverse ideas have been produced even within the conventionally framed European history. Some of the most persistent ideas and ideals are ones which have outlived their usefulness, others have not. Nietzsche explores the European legacy in order to come up with a view of philosophy and life that does not divorce reason and desire, one which acknowledges personal and cultural change, one which considers the holding of values a necessary preliminary to assertions about facts. He finds such ideas in places as diverse as ancient Greek culture and the moral philosophy of eighteenth-century France. Nietzsche then begins his own task of reclamation which includes a critique of some philosophical and cultural practices. Philosophy, as he sees it, comes to involve the creative involvement of a whole person. The metaphors Nietzsche uses involve passion, movement, excitement, and interest. The ideas of life and experience form an important part of Nietzsche's work. They are the keys to understanding his unconventional demands on the history of philosophy.

Nietzsche is an unconventional thinker in that he both acknowledges cultural historical changes and resists putting these changes into a formula. For Nietzsche, what may be required for a specific age and place will not necessarily be helpful to another. There is no pattern to historical movement. There is nothing to comfort us, nothing certain, nothing to make us more secure. This openness with respect to history is not something that is likely to make him popular with other philosophers. He rejects what they most often take to be their chief attributes and distinguishing characteristics: the special place of the logical faculty, the "fact" that their truths are ahistorical or asocial, and the justification of the empirical method. The task of the philosopher must be explored in a time when metaphysics has become suspect and then impossible, and at a time when the tasks of philosophy have turned epistemological, have turned in upon themselves to examine the knower and the knower's relation to the known.

The modern period's usual solution to this dilemma was to turn to empiricism and positive science. Yet, at a time when the methods of positive science were fast becoming the norm of European intellectual models, Nietzsche was already criticizing them as atavistic. According to him, their goals were related to previous metaphysical aims. The practitioners of such philosophies had not been sufficiently rigorous in their critiques. For Nietzsche; truth, knowledge, and certainty give way to value making. Even scientific knowledge is evaluated psychologically and pragmatically in terms of physiology or pathology. This is all a consequence of giving up the possibility of a transcendental perspective. Nietzsche makes a move to an understanding of involved experience or a situated perspective. The world of our experience is the subject matter of philosophy.

When Nietzsche turns to questions of moral value in philosophy, he says that "sitting in moral judgment should offend our taste." Our taste is part of who we are, it gives color to existence. It sets the stamp of our personalities on our actions. There is something distasteful about "sitting in judgment." Nietzsche is suspicious of the removal of the judge and about the petty interest in evaluating someone else's actions. This offends his taste. Nietzsche's critique of philosophy attempts to eliminate this perspective and all the views that imitated it whether consciously or unconsciously. Most Western morality has adopted the perspective of a judge. The model for the "fair" passing of judgment in the moral and political context of contemporary culture is one where the judges are believed to be uninvolved in the situation about which they must judge. Nietzsche believes this model exists because of the perseverance of the belief in transcendental model which existed in metaphysics. In Greek and

European metaphysics there was an example of an all-knowing or all-good judge. Now that possibility has been abandoned, and it is necessary to consider alternative models of valuation. Nietzsche's genealogy of contemporary moral values accounts for how our values came to be. Nietzsche must then go beyond contemporary models of evaluation. His own morality, which goes beyond good and evil, is one such attempt.

What Nietzsche has to say in a positive sense, he gets from Greek antiquity. Nietzsche uses his reading of antiquity as a model of how to live. Classical studies are "untimely" because they are different from our time. It is because of this that they have such a precious value for us. In Greek culture and philosophy Nietzsche finds an emphasis on the relation of knowledge to the experience of living. He thinks that this demand should be made on the philosophy and philology of his day. Nietzsche reclaims these ideas for philosophy with the expectation that they will bring an infusion of refreshing ideas. These ideas are much needed in contemporary European culture because of its dismal and pessimistic Christian world view.

Along with this reclamation, Nietzsche has also sought an example or a metaphor for our everyday creativity. This is the creativity which constitutes us as persons. So, to the demand for vitality from Antiquity is added the experience of the artist with its openness, and its power to transform. Nietzsche wants an aesthetic revolution as well as a philosophical one. In fact, it would be more correct to say that the philosophical (methodological), aesthetic, and moral are part of the same revolution.

This book addresses Nietzsche's analysis of the end of metaphysics, which he saw as the theoretical consequence of the death of the Christian God. The philosophical positions of intellectual disinterest and objectivity are also casualties of this death. There are, also, serious consequences for moral values which come with the perspective change from transcendence to an immanence. One consequence was the need for an alternative account of how the beliefs we have came into place. Nietzsche employs a genealogical method for understanding the moral systems we have inherited. As we have seen, Nietzsche returned to his philological studies of ancient Greece in order to find confirmation of his own view that a philosophy can exist which incorporates all aspects of our lives. He was interested in reclaiming an attitude which was very much a part of these views and something Nietzsche seemed to value very much personally. This attitude was opposed to the dogmatic and transcendental trends Nietzsche found prevalent in most of the philosophy of his day. It was the attempt, achieved by method and style, to infuse vitality, life, and joy into the tasks of morality, artistic creation, and knowing. In our culture, the last remnant of affirmative expression is found in artistic creation. In other areas dogmatism has carried the day. So Nietzsche tries to look to art when he searches for a model of living and evaluation that will avoid the pessimism of the past by being open to all aspects of life. The consequences of what he finds are then applied to the most important areas of human understanding: morality and epistemology. These are the areas he considers the most vital to human living and hence to philosophical thought.

All work is to a certain extent collaborative. Over the years I have benefited from the thoughts and critical comments of many colleagues and students. It is only possible to mention some of them here. I would like to credit conversations which have spanned a decade with Alexander Nehamas and the late John Atwell. Their generosity, kindness, and professionalism have been very important to me. My much loved colleagues at Earlham College—Liffey Thorpe, Peter Suber, Bob Horn, John Newman, and Paul Lacey—have challenged my readings of Nietzsche. They have, in some cases, even challenged whether or not I should be reading Nietzsche. I thank them for their concern, respect and intelligent criticism. Earlham College and the University of Southern Maine have given me the opportunity to offer seminars on Nietzsche's philosophy and its impact on social and cultural practices. Students and colleagues in these classes have wrestled with complex and subtle questions of interpretation and with questions of the cultural legacy of the thinker. At the University of Southern Maine, Julien Murphy of the Philosophy Department and Dean Richard Stebbins of the College of Arts and Sciences have been particularly supportive of my work.

Special thanks go to my editors Robert Ginsberg and H. G. Callaway. It is a privilege to work with such energetic, exacting, and kind-spirited people. Jeannette Haas compiled most of the index, and worked tirelessly on formatting the text and editing. Kay Dudley, a philosophy student, has provided significant research and editorial work. Marguerite Roosen proofread the manuscript and provided much good-natured support during the completion of the book. Although I acknowledge the support from all of these fine people, any errors in the final text are my own responsibility. Finally, I would like to thank Claire and Jeff, who make it all worthwhile.

INTRODUCTION

> We knowers are unknown to ourselves, and for a good reason: how can we ever hope to find what we have never looked for? There is a sound adage which runs: "Where a man's treasure lies, there lies his heart." Our treasure lies in the beehives of our knowledge. We are perpetually on our way thither, being by nature winged insects and honey gatherers of the mind. The only thing that lies close to our heart is the desire to bring something home to the hive. *As for the rest of life—so-called "experience"—who among us is serious enough for that?* Or has time enough? When it comes to such matters, our heart is not in it—we don't even lend our ear.[1]

This book is about the reclamation of philosophy. It is a hermeneutical interpretation of Friedrich Nietzsche's philosophy. The purpose of the interpretation is to understand what Nietzsche meant philosophy to be, particularly what he meant it to be in relation to our lives. For Nietzsche, a philosophy which could not be lived had no meaning or it had a quaint meaning with respect to our understanding of the personality who created it. Nietzsche felt that a lived philosophy needed to be reclaimed because he believed that philosophy, especially as it was alienated from our actual experience, was in need of being reevaluated. Nietzsche believed that philosophy needed to be rescued from its unhealthy and undesirable state. He wanted it to be brought to a state of literacy, culture, and health.

A certain type of philosophy had come to the end of its usefulness. This should not sound strange to our ears for we have heard it from Martin Heidegger and Richard Rorty,[2] to name but two. Heidegger is directly influenced by Nietzsche, although it is customary to make more of the influence of Edmund Husserl on his work. His two-volume work[3] on Nietzsche attests to the fact that he takes Nietzsche seriously as a "thinker." A "thinker" for Heidegger is a "post-philosophy" philosopher. Nietzsche also believes himself to be a "post-philosophy" philosopher but, unlike Heidegger, he is unwilling to give up the word or title; instead, he invests it with new meaning.

Much of philosophy, especially that dominated by an interest in linear logic, is committed to a conception of the discipline as engaged primarily in argumentation. There are certain "logical" or "rational" arguments present in texts and it is the job of the philosopher to find these, to represent them, and then to find out if they are sound. Not only do many contemporary philosophers aim for the creation of texts whose arguments are free from gaping holes of logic; they also read the history of philosophy as a history of persons who had similar interests and aims. At least they believe that if this history is to be considered valuable in a contemporary context it needs to be treated as if such activities were its aim. If this is not the case, so they would argue, then such philosophy has only interest to the antiquarian or intellectual historian, not to the philosopher, properly speaking. Nietzsche was attacking this view of philosophy as he saw it arising in its nascent form, in the late nineteenth century.

If philosophy is not necessarily about logic and not exclusively concerned with reason, then what is it about? This is a question which is of special concern for philosophers who believe they have a stake in preserving the uniqueness of their discipline. Nietzsche did not care much about the lines of the disciplines. Perhaps this was because he was trained as a philologist instead of as a philosopher and is therefore unattached to maintaining the purity of the latter profession. But in his writings on philology he exhibits the same disinterest in drawing disciplinary lines. Nietzsche is concerned with the question of disciplines only insofar as he is concerned with the philosophy's transformation.

For Nietzsche, philosophy was many things, but it was always interpretation. Often the "text" which was interpreted was the life and mores of his culture. The strategy of interpretation was to understand in a historical and cultural context, often by comparing the contemporary values of his culture to those of other cultures. For Nietzsche, philosophy is not about argumentation, it is about interpretation; it is not about knowledge, it is about understanding. I might go farther and say that it is not about truth, it is about honesty. These ideas need to be explored more fully, and they will be in the main body of this text.

Nietzsche thought that a great deal of Western philosophy is concerned with things which are not terribly important and that we live in a time when we cannot afford the luxury of ignoring issues of vital importance. Some of these issues in contemporary Western culture have been approached, using Nietzsche's methodology. Michel Foucault's analyses of prisons and mental institutions, Cornel West's analysis of "racism," and Kathryn Pyne Parson Addelson's analysis of the late nineteenth-century American feminist moral revolution all address issues of vital cultural importance. These are issues which should not just be of concern to the sociologist, because the way they are approached methodologically will suggest different methods or strategies for change. What is needed, in the evaluation of this variety of methods, is the sophistication of the philosopher. This will be seen below when I examine the way in which both Kathryn Addelson and Cornel West use some aspects of Nietzsche's philosophy.

Nietzsche believed that the collapse of Christian metaphysics is a momentous event and the job of reconstructing an ethic for only oneself is a difficult, challenging, and exhilarating task. There are also things in Nietzsche with which I cannot agree, some of which are really abhorrent: his chauvinism of every kind, his contemptuous and unfair treatment of many philosophers and writers, his occasional overly heroic conception of the individual—as either moral agent or artist. The latter is the only one with which this work is directly concerned. Rather than take time to refute the other issues here, like Nietzsche, I will lay these matters aside. He says, "One refutes a matter by laying it respectfully on ice— To ignore something is sometimes the most powerful and effective refutation."[4] Not, in this case, because the refutation was not needed, but instead because it has already been done *ad nauseam*.

The Nietzsche I am interested in reclaiming is Nietzsche the philosopher. We will look at Nietzsche's ideas about some new philosophical methodologies, and at his view of life-experience. This will involve looking at his critique of previous philosophy. Only if we see the extent of that critique will we see why Nietzsche believed that there was no alternative but to experiment with new or reclaimed methods and ideas. Some of these methods are quite different from those practiced by Nietzsche's contemporaries (whether they be philosophers or philologists). But ultimately we must get past this and look at what Nietzsche did finally reach: the reclamation or transfiguration of philosophy. Because he used a number of aesthetic models for that view, this work will also end on the topic of art. Nietzsche's view of the artist as a creator within a cultural context provides us with one model. Another comes from our understanding of the way aesthetic values change over larger historical periods.

The philosophy of which Nietzsche is critical is characterized by belief in a conception of reason which allows for transcendence and autonomy: Nietzsche does not believe this is possible. Such a conception is characterized by a belief in logic, and logic rests on the idea of there being identical cases: Nietzsche says that it therefore rests on a falsification of experience (that is, in experience there are only similar cases). Unlike reason, which has its good and bad forms, Nietzsche doesn't have a good word to say about logic.

Another problem with philosophy, a related one, is that it has a tendency to divorce whatever is under consideration (for example, a value) from its context. This tendency creates an abstraction or reduction which produces a distorted view of that thing or value. It does this while, at the same time, claiming that the view is free from distortion.

In this quotation from *The Genealogy of Morals* Nietzsche gives us a quick summary of what he wants to reclaim for philosophy. I will consider it in detail further on in this work.

> Let us, from now on be on our guard against the hallowed philosophers' myth of a "pure, will-less, painless, timeless knower"; let us beware of the tentacles of such contradictory notions as "pure reason," "absolute knowledge," "absolute intelligence." All these concepts presuppose an eye such as no living being can imagine, an eye required to have no direction, to abrogate its active and interpretative powers—precisely those powers that alone make of seeing, seeing *something*. All seeing is essentially perspective, and so is all knowing. The more emotions we allow to speak in a given matter, the more different eyes we can put on in order to view a given spectacle, the more complete will be our conception of it, the greater our "objectivity." But to eliminate the will, to suspend the emotions altogether, provided it could be done—surely this would be to castrate the intellect, would it not?[5]

We begin to see here that hermeneutical interpretative powers require a knower who is whole. A quite new, quite different kind of philosophy is going to be necessary; a philosophy with a different conception of the knower and of knowing.

These are criticisms of characteristics which are quite basic to Western philosophy. Because of these criticisms and other more favorable evaluations concerning what is desirable in philosophies of the past, Nietzsche finds it necessary to look for a new method or a new style. We will see this in his treatments of Heraclitus, some French moral philosophers, and even, to a certain extent, some English historians of morals. Nietzsche seeks a new method or style; in this respect he is not so very different from Husserl and many other innovative philosophers. Husserl called himself a perpetual beginner. He was always trying a new method to help him arrive at his peculiarly phenomenological notion of objectivity. What is peculiar about Nietzsche is that he went so far afield (that is, from more widely practiced traditional philosophical methodologies) in his attempt to find a method which was free from some of the "errors" of previous philosophy. This is because he wanted a philosophy which did not do violence to what I will call life-experience.

Nietzsche tried on many styles, many masks, as it has become fashionable to call them. He uses aphorisms, parables, little histories, hyperbole, and *ad hominem* attacks, to name but a few of his styles and techniques. He does this for many reasons. Nietzsche's aim is to wake up philosophy. Philosophy should arise out of "its dogmatic slumber," if I may borrow a phrase from one of his most ill treated opponents. Nietzsche does this in part by violating certain expected academic conventions.

Philosophy is not merely dead because its methods are archaic and have ceased to serve a useful function in society. Nietzsche believes it is dead because it refuses to condescend to deal with issues which arise out of life. It refuses to take seriously the moral values which have to do with the very "small" everyday decisions which we make. It refuses to acknowledge the way what we believe and value is attached to how we form our taste in the structuring of our environment. To counter this lack, Nietzsche says we "want to be the poets of our life—first of all in the smallest, most everyday matters."[6] What we want to do is create values and create a culture. This is one of the tasks of the tragic (euphoric?) philosopher.[7]

Nietzsche wants us to break out of both the methodological and substantial conventions of philosophy. He shows this in a variety of ways. The writings of a few French thinkers provide him with some of his models. His admiration for French moralists, who use the aphoristic style, is described quite accurately by Brendan Donnellan in his book *Nietzsche and the French Moralists.*

> What Nietzsche admired in these moralists was above all their strength and fullness as truly *personal* rather than "objectively detached" thinkers: "... all the great French connoisseurs of men, from Montaigne, Charron, and La Rochefoucauld down to Chamfort and Stendhal, possessed their own will and character within themselves." ... Integrity, the will to expose the comfortable lies from which popular myths are woven, and

> the fortitude necessary to bear the harsh truths thus revealed, were the fundamental prerequisites of Nietzsche's revolutionary philosophy. In the French moralists he found intellectual guides and personal models equal to these demands.[8]

The methods which were attractive to Nietzsche were ones which, to use his phrase, "served life." For him, intellectual and philosophical activity had to do with the construction of yourself as a moral and aesthetic being. This meant constructing your taste and molding your actions. It required models as examples, but not laws demanding conformity.

Some of the methods Nietzsche uses are not so terribly radical, especially not to the twentieth-century ear. The genealogy, as we will see, has its antecedents in "good" philology, in "bad" (that is, British) histories of morality, and in contemporary critiques of Christian morality. These judgments or opinions are "good" and "bad" according to Nietzsche, but there are at least some philosophical or academic antecedents to much of Nietzsche's methodology.

Another of Nietzsche's methods, again by no means new, is the use of the aphorism. Let us discuss this method first. Although this interpretation does not rely heavily on aphorisms, something which Nietzsche says about the interpretation of aphorisms is essential to this account. It will help us to understand the structure of the argument in each chapter of this work. Nietzsche says the following about his own interpretation of an aphorism.

> ... the aphoristic form may present a stumbling block, the difficulty being that this form is no longer taken "hard" enough. An aphorism that has been honestly struck cannot be deciphered simply by reading it off; this is only the beginning of the work of interpretation proper, which requires a whole science of hermeneutics. In the third essay of this book [*The Genealogy of Morals*] I give an example of what I mean by true interpretation: an aphorism stands at the head of that essay, and the body of the essay forms the commentary. One skill is needed—lost today, unfortunately—for the practice of reading as an art: the skill to ruminate, which cows possess but modern man lacks. This is why my writings will, for some time yet, remain difficult to digest.[9]

We need to take Nietzsche seriously with regard to what he says about hermeneutical interpretation. Each chapter of this book begins with a quotation. It is not necessarily an aphorism, but it is a pithy remark whose meaning is somewhat obscure. In the course of the chapter we will explore the general issue which the quotation raises. Each chapter ends with an interpretation of the quotation in the light of what we have explored. Thus Nietzsche's conception of one way to do philosophy is used in order to create an interpretation and understanding of his own work.

Again, to the modern ear the vagaries of hermeneutics are nothing new. We live in an age which is re-examining some of the interpretive works of Wilhelm Dilthey and Hans-Georg Gadamer. Some of the criticisms which Nietzsche has received are the same as those which have been leveled at the science or discipline of hermeneutics (for example, that it is not philosophy or not a science). Nietzsche was exploring what possibilities were left after his extremely extensive critique of previous philosophies and their methodologies. He believes that we have to engage in these new interpretative and critical techniques because the other options have been exhausted. The main point of the beginnings of the first two chapters of this work is to rehearse those objections in order to see why Nietzsche believes he is compelled to abandon such a large portion of Western philosophy and its methodology. We are not taking issue with Nietzsche's interpretation of the history of philosophy. This has been done elsewhere—by other commentators on Nietzsche. The point is to find the reason Nietzsche believes he is compelled to explore the very different methodologies he uses. I must emphasize that Nietzsche believed that it was tragic to lose so much philosophy, but he also believed in the power and correctness of his own critique. Thus he considered the loss inevitable.

In the nineteenth century, perhaps the most startling aspect of Nietzsche's philosophy was the death of the Christian God. But to us in the twentieth century, it is instead our realization of how far beyond the death of God Nietzsche went. We now accept the death of God as an unquestioned and uninteresting fact, that is, in at least one of the ways in which Nietzsche meant it. Judeo-Christian theology does not constitute our world view. It does not have the place it once had in our culture. If it did, we would go to priests for aid instead of to doctors and psychologists, etc. With the exception of a few pockets of enthusiasm, this idea considered in the full extent of its metaphysical meaning is largely dead in Western culture. It has been replaced by positivism and "science" in the larger culture.

What intrigues us today about Nietzsche is how far beyond his time he really was; this posthumous thinker. The death of God went so deeply into his soul partially because he saw the "tragedy" of such a loss, but also because he understood the connection between the various beliefs which form the basis for our culture. This is something which in the twentieth century we do not understand well enough. We are interested in separating and professionalizing knowledge: in specialized knowledge. Nietzsche was still among the thinkers who looked at connections between disciplines and ideas, especially those which were embedded in history. He did not merely look for connections which were embedded in logic.

In Nietzsche's views on metaphysics, epistemology, ethics, and aesthetics we can explore the depth of his critique of philosophy. The consequences of the collapse of an other-worldly perspective will be explored. In each case there is a move from the perspective of a "disinterested" judge of truth and value to a view of the knower or valuer as a participant in the process. The knower is involved and interested. It is this which is the consequence of the death of God. Because the death of God is the death of all transcendence, it is the death of the possibility of judgment from the outside. In his early notes Nietzsche says:

> What does truth matter to man? The highest and purest life is possible with the belief that one possesses the truth. Man requires *belief in truth*. Truth makes its appearance as a social necessity. Afterwards, by means of a metastasis it is applied to everything, where it is not required. All virtues arise from pressing needs. The necessity for truthfulness begins with society. Otherwise man dwells within eternal concealments. The establishment of states promotes truthfulness. The drive toward knowledge has a moral origin.[10]

The idea of transcendence gives way to perspective. We find that values are foundational, not "found." As a "foundation" they are "willed" or sustained by belief.

Because Nietzsche criticizes what lies at the heart of a great deal of academic philosophy, it is common for him to be dismissed, for him not to be considered a philosopher. This is also true because of what he embraces. We can see this in an early influential study by Crane Brinton first published in 1941 in the Harvard "Makers of Modern Europe Series." This is a biographical series which addresses "What was the significance of this man for his epoch."[11] Brinton's answers to that question is that Nietzsche's followers find: aesthetic enjoyment, a social study of human behavior, or a new religion.[12] What they fail to find is a philosopher. Instead, they find an artist, a sociologist, or an idol. Until comparatively recent times, especially in America (the European response, as we shall see, is quite another story), this denial of his philosophical importance is common.

The failure to take Nietzsche seriously as a philosophical thinker resulted in a very superficial view of his work. Brinton's Nietzsche was a madman who engaged in contradiction and who although not himself a fascist left the world ripe for the Nazis.[13] He is a radical who proposes immoderate and dangerous ideas. Brinton says, "Nietzsche, wherever he led, did not lead towards the Rights of Man."[14] Nietzsche would to a certain extent agree with this interpretation. He would, in spite of other disagreements, agree with Jeremy Bentham that "Rights" are nonsense on stilts. But, this does not mean he had no feeling for the issues which discussions on rights usually raise. Other readers do not find him so uncongenial, and even find or emphasize more liberal statements in his work. For example, Brinton might be surprised to find Nietzsche saying:

> Dying for the "truth."—We should not let ourselves be burnt for our opinions: we are not that sure of them. But perhaps for this: that we may have and change our opinions.[15]

This is not an idea one commonly associates with Nietzsche.

Although Brinton admits that his is not a philosophical treatment, he still does not find Nietzsche to be a major philosophical influence on his "epoch."

Instead Brinton sees Nietzsche's main contribution to "the science of sociology" where:

> Nietzsche made no inconsiderable contribution to the study of how men behave, and more particularly to the study of the relation between their actual behavior and their professed beliefs and systems of belief, their religions, ethics, philosophies.[16]

Although this is certainly true of Nietzsche, this type of analysis ignores the critiques of previous philosophy. This in turn has the consequence of making it difficult to see his philosophy as a philosophy at all.

Mary Agnes Hamilton, although otherwise a sympathetic reader, echoes this common criticism:

> Nietzsche thought of himself as a constructive philosopher, and some of his solemn admirers have endeavored, with more than German thoroughness, to present him in that light. He was not. He was a man of extraordinary intellectual curiosity, power and courage, of great originality, of remarkable insight and candour: and a poet. But in the strict sense, the only sense that matters, he was not a philosopher.[17]

But we must look at the reasons Hamilton gives: "His thought is human, not abstract: its motive aesthetic, not metaphysical." Humanity and aesthetics are precisely the qualities which Nietzsche wanted to see used to transform philosophy. Consider Nietzsche's "definition" of philosophy from the preface to the second edition of *The Gay Science.*

> A philosopher who has traversed many kinds of health, and keeps traversing them, has passed through an equal number of philosophies; he simply cannot keep from transposing his states every time into the most spiritual form and distance: this art of transfiguration is philosophy. We philosophers are not free to divide body from soul as the people do; we are even less free to divide soul from spirit ....
> Life—that means for us constantly transforming all that we are into light and flame.[18]

It is Brinton's Nietzsche, and other even less favorable accounts, which Walter Kaufmann wanted to put to rest. Kaufmann successfully fought the view of Nietzsche the fascist, and the equally dismissive view of Nietzsche the romantic artist and Greco-phile. He made Nietzsche respectable in certain more scholarly (especially American) philosophical circles. Not surprisingly, this was at a cost to Nietzsche. In Kaufmann's concern to establish Nietzsche as a philosopher, certain features of his work were best overlooked. The hyperbole and the *ad hominem* attacks name but two. Kaufmann describes the book

Zarathustra in the "Introduction" to his translation:

> Rhapsody, satire, and epigram predominate; but Nietzsche's mature thought is clouded and shrouded by an excess of adolescent emotion. Nevertheless despite the all-too-human self-pity and occasional bathos, the book is full of fascinating ideas; and probably it owes its unique success with the broad mass of readers not least to its worst qualities.[19]

These "worst qualities" are some of the things for which Jacques Derrida, for example, likes him. These are seen in Derrida's view as part of Nietzsche's philosophy, not as unfortunate overindulgences.

The Nietzsche we find in Derrida's *Spurs* is the playful celebrant of sexuality, provocation, and ambiguity. These qualities are certainly found in Nietzsche's work. They are found in *Zarathustra* in "the Other Dancing Song," for example. Derrida gives us the vibrant Nietzsche—the alive one. I will return to a discussion of some aspects of Derrida's Nietzsche further along.

Kaufmann says that Nietzsche's "concern was primarily with the individual who is not satisfied with accepted formulas."[20] While this is quite true, this "individual" is in a culture and Nietzsche does not forget that for a moment, even though at times he must emphasize the individual in order to talk about creating against a culture. Consideration of this point forms the focus of the chapters on aesthetics.

Kaufmann makes Nietzsche more acceptable. He gets him philosophical status in the history of the discipline as a substantial thinker. Arthur Danto is in turn effective in getting Nietzsche to be taken seriously among a group of philosophers who are extremely unlikely to find him congenial, namely, Analytic philosophers. Danto makes Nietzsche into someone more likely to be of interest to an analytic philosopher, by promoting an interpretation of Nietzsche's work that emphasizes ideas which can be translated into problems of contemporary analytic philosophy.

Danto takes ideas in Nietzsche's works and makes concepts of them. In his hands, "Perspectivism" and "Transfiguration," words which Nietzsche seldom uses, are concretized. Nietzsche does not give definitions of concepts and then repeat them as formulas. He attempts to keep his writing fluid and natural. The other type of writing and thinking is something which he intentionally avoided,[21] and which he often associates with dogmatism.

Danto does emphasize the importance of the aesthetic in Nietzsche's thought but, as with Kaufmann discussed above, he believes (if we are to judge by what he does) that what is philosophically interesting is often best found by taking it out of its stylistic context.

The radical character of Nietzsche's thought, even in its first significant expression, may be seen in the fact that he is indeed prepared to allow that art has no less claim to truth than sense or science to objective truth.[22] He goes on to say that this is because the latter two do not lead to objective truth either. Instead, they leave us with illusions. Danto made Nietzsche pleasing to the analytic palate, but there is a lot of Nietzsche not there, or there is not much of Nietzsche there.

This interpretation emphasizes the fact that Nietzsche is resistant to "isms" and formulas without being an individualist. This resistance forms part of the reason for people saying that he is not a philosopher. Theories and formulas are what is expected from a philosopher. Nietzsche's philosophy is both curious and interesting precisely because he sees the weaknesses in a number of versions of philosophy which have had this as their goal. Yet he still wants to be a philosopher and thinks there is something meaningful about philosophical activity.

One of the other methods which Nietzsche uses he calls a genealogy. This will be discussed at greater length below but, for now, let us consider a few of its features and explain why this method is important. This interpretation of Nietzsche's philosophy rests on the importance, the centrality, of a few texts. This is because of their methodology. These texts are *The Birth of Tragedy* and *On the Genealogy of Morals*. In both of these works there is an emphasis on a social cultural understanding of value. In the earlier work the focus is on aesthetic value, in the latter it is on moral value.

Both of these accounts are taken to be genealogical. They are historical explorations and interpretations. Both of them aim at a reevaluation of a contemporary style of art or style of life. It is this peculiar aspect of Nietzsche's work which has captured the imagination of so many French writers, for example: Michel Foucault, Sarah Kofman, Luce Irigaray; and so few Americans. To have some sense of the difference of reception, consider Maurice Merleau-Ponty's comment in "Eye and Mind" from *The Primacy of Perception*, "when the lowliest student, ever since Nietzsche, would flatly reject philosophy if it did not teach how to live fully [à être des grands vivants]."[23] Even in 1961 this aspect of Nietzsche's thought was quite influential in France.

Nietzsche might speak in his own defense here. His reception among Americans is very much what he might have anticipated. In *The Gay Science* §329 Nietzsche discusses some characteristics of Americans. These have a point in Nietzsche's social critiques. He talks about the "breathless haste" with which we work and how we make a virtue of that "vice." "Even now one is ashamed of resting, and prolonged reflection almost gives people a bad conscience." He goes on:

> One thinks with a watch in one's hand, even as one eats one's midday meal while reading the latest news of the stock market; one lives as if one always might "miss out on something." ... the universal demand for *gross obviousness in* all those situations in which human beings wish to be honest with one another for once....
> Living in a constant chase after gain compels people to extend their spirit to the point of exhaustion in continual pretense and overreaching and anticipating others. Virtue has come to consist of doing something in less time than someone else.

> Hours in which honesty is *permitted* have become very rare, and when they arrive one is tired and does not want to "let oneself go" but actually wishes to *stretch out* as long and wide and ungainly as one happens to be.
>
> More and more, *work* enlists all good conscience on its side; the desire for joy already calls itself a "need to recuperate" and is beginning to be ashamed of itself. "One owes it to one's health"—that is what people say when they are caught on an excursion into the country. Soon we may well reach the point where people can no longer give in to the desire for a *vita contemplativa* (that is, taking a walk with ideas and friends) without self-contempt and a bad conscience.[24]

Philosophy too must be liberated from this "gross" and dismal seriousness.

In the work of Michel Foucault it is easy to see the legacy of Nietzsche's genealogical method. Foucault is a man who read the following passage from *The Gay Science* and took it seriously. Now Nietzsche could finally rest with a successor who was not a disciple, a worthy successor. The passage from Nietzsche reads as follows:

> *Something for the Industrious.*— Anyone who now wishes to make a study of moral matters opens up for himself an immense field for work. All kinds of individual passions have to be thought through and pursued through different ages, peoples, and great and small individuals; all their reason and all their evaluations and perspectives on things have to be brought into the light. So far, all that has given color to existence still lacks a history. Where could you find a history of love, of avarice, of envy, of conscience, of pious respect for tradition, or of cruelty? Even a comparative history of law or at least of punishment is so far lacking completely.
>
> Whatever men have so far viewed as the conditions of their existence—and all the reason, passion, and superstition involved in such a view—has this been researched exhaustively? The most industrious people will find that it involves too much work simply to observe how differently men's instincts have grown, and might yet grow, depending on different moral climates.... And it would be yet another job to determine the erroneousness of all these reasons and the whole nature of moral judgments to date.
>
> If all these jobs were done, the most insidious question of all would emerge into the foreground: whether science [*Wissenschaft*] can furnish goals of action after it has proved that it can take such goals away and annihilate them; ... So far, science [*Wissenschaft*] has not yet built its cyclopic buildings; but the time for that, too, will come.[25]

Nietzsche wrote a number of these histories. Surely *The Genealogy of Morals* addresses some of the suggested topics: for example, an exploration of punishment and of asceticism. In Foucault's work they are carried out further. Foucault has, in fact, been quite frank in acknowledging Nietzsche's influence upon him.[26]

To return to the genealogy, there are a number of stories which we could tell about the way the world is and why we have certain beliefs and practices. It is the latter question, the one involving evaluation, which intrigues Nietzsche. People give value and meaning to their existence. The consideration of people as value givers and value makers is what he finds interesting. In a sense his work is psychological. He is interested in examining the motivations which lie behind our value creations. The emphasis in most of his work is not on our individual creations and the answers to questions of values which we find in our actions. If it were, he might have only written fiction or been merely a psychologist. The emphasis is instead on seeing these views as social forces. In this respect Brinton is quite right about Nietzsche and his importance: Nietzsche is, or could be, extremely vital to sociology.

Cornel West has written, in addition to the article mentioned above, an excellent article called "The Genealogy of Racism: On the Underside of Modern Discourse."[27] In this article West describes himself as using the genealogical method advocated and practiced by Nietzsche and Foucault. This returns us to the question of why Nietzsche and this reclamation are seen as necessarily philosophical instead of, for example, sociological. This is why we need philosophers to address the social concerns of our time.

West is critical (although not dismissive) of orthodox Marxist or liberal solutions to the problem of "Racism" in America and elsewhere. His point is not that the analyses and recommendations for solutions are entirely wrong. It is instead that they "insure an easy resolution to a complex problem." They do this:

> ... without calling into question certain fundamental assumptions which inform such resolutions. These fundamental assumptions, such as the subject-based conception of power, and easy resolutions, such as the elimination of race prejudice by knowledge or the abolition of racism under socialism, preclude theoretical alternatives and strategic options.[28]

The various accounts of "Racism" in contemporary culture lead to different strategies for dealing with them. West as a philosopher has the sophistication to see the outcomes of these views. Resisting the easy and inadequate solutions offered by liberalism and Marxism he looks for "the emergence [*Entstehung*] or the 'moment of arising' of the idea of white supremacy within the modern discourse of the West."[29]

We look for the particular brand of inequality called "Racism" in the discourse which produced the concept of "race" as a scientific classification. West finds that the model of white supremacy is to be found in the "scientific" and theoretically unbiased system of classification which produced the idea of races. We will not take the time to rehearse West's argument here. The point is that seeing the tie between theory and practice is vital for facilitating social change. West's account makes visible a number of cultural biases against blacks which are invisible under the liberal and Marxist frameworks. For example, he finds historical reasons for the bias against black equality in beauty and culture.

Let us now consider a much earlier article by Kathryn Addelson (then Kathryn Pyne Parsons), "Nietzsche and Moral Change."[30] In this work Nietzsche's methodology, and especially his view of moral change or revolution, is compared to Paul Feyerabend's and Thomas Kuhn's views of scientific revolution. For our purposes this is not as meaningful as her use of Nietzsche's idea of moral change as a model for understanding what went on in the feminist "revolutions" of the late nineteenth and early twentieth centuries. Like Foucault she uses this particular historical case to argue for an understanding of morality, and more specifically of "moral creativity." She writes in the beginning of her article:

> By paying attention to moral revolution, Nietzsche was able to understand ... (that "moral creativity" did not make sense within a theory of morality which is exhausted by notions of obligation, principle, and justification). I'd like to work with his insights and develop some of the points I think he was trying to make. This means that I shall not be doing "Nietzsche scholarship" but rather trying to apply some of his insights to theoretical and practical problems which face us. Given his views on the interpretation of literature, I don't believe this is against the Nietzschean spirit.[31]

Addelson's approach is not against the spirit of what Nietzsche is doing either. In fact Nietzsche's understanding of life (as essentially involving change and becoming) is one of the more exciting aspects of his work. This idea of moral change, or moral revolution as Addelson calls it, puts the idea of something's coming into being in the context of the other thing which Nietzsche was most concerned with: value.

Cornel West and Kathryn Addelson both use Nietzsche in a way in which he would find methodologically congenial. Rather than stopping with an analysis or interpretation of his work they, like Foucault, go on to do what Nietzsche recommends. Combating "racism" or explicating feminist history are not activities which Nietzsche would seem likely to have chosen for his subjects, although it is interesting that we find Nietzsche being used by feminists and socialists even in his lifetime. It is unfortunate that so much has been written about Stefan George and other "cult of the individual" types of writers, and so little about writers like Havelock Ellis, Mary Agnes Hamilton, Edith Ellis, Georg Simmel, and Helene Stöcker who give us a more interesting range of views on Nietzsche as a social thinker and reformer.[32]

As we have seen, Derrida and Foucault could hardly be accused of finding the same Nietzsche. But, they are alike in reclaiming for philosophy those parts of Nietzsche which other readers (although they may find them amusing or interesting) do not find philosophical. Derrida does not ignore the Nietzsche who plays and who thinks playing is a part of knowing. Mary Agnes Hamilton is also sympathetic to this aspect of Nietzsche's work. In her article "Nietzsche: The Laughing Philosopher" she writes:

> Nietzsche believed, profoundly, in laughter; the power to laugh was, for him, the final mark of the noble man and he himself laughs constantly: the whole of his writing is interpenetrated and coloured by it. The things he laughs at are infinitely various.... His humour is not compartmented: it plays over everything: it breaks across his most impassioned seriousness and is a part of it, its essence and flavour.[33]

Hamilton is interested in emphasizing an aspect of Nietzsche's work which is so often ignored or insufficiently considered (one might add enjoyed). She goes on to elucidate the danger which might come out of such neglect.

> The reader who takes his [Nietzsche's] words literally, without perceiving that they are shot by this double colouring, naturally makes nonsense of them, as so many readers have done. He cannot be taken literally. He is nearly always ironical. Irony is the form in which the sense of humour of a hard mind naturally expresses itself: and Nietzsche had a hard mind, if ever there was one. His heart was not hard ....[34]

The playfulness and light in Nietzsche's philosophy is one of the things which Derrida finds congenial to his own attempt to transform philosophy and "serious" academic thinking.

Nietzsche tells us a bit more about what it is to be a philosopher. Let us return to a passage from *The Gay Science* quoted above. We still have that idea of passion undisguised which is to be a part of the philosopher's relation to work and to life. This is a relation which again stresses the creative involvement of a whole person.

> We philosophers are not free to divide body from soul as the people do; we are even less free to divide soul from spirit.... Life—that means for us constantly transforming all that we are into light and flame.[35]

The metaphors Nietzsche uses involve passion, movement, excitement, and interest.

The ideas of life and experience form such an integral part of Nietzsche's work. In fact, they are the keys to understanding his unconventional demands on the history of philosophy. But, again, Nietzsche is not alone in both speaking about existence and realizing the difficulty or ambiguity in so doing. Søren Kierkegaard faces a similar difficulty in some of his work. The following is from his *The Concluding Unscientific Postscript*:

> If the concept of existence is really to be stressed, this cannot be given a direct expression as a paragraph in a system; all direct swearing and oath supported assurances serve only to make the topsy-turvy profession of the paragraph more ridiculous. An actual emphasis on existence must be expressed in an essential form; in view of the elusiveness of existence, such a form will have an indirect form, namely, the absence of a system. But this again must not degenerate into an asseverating formula, for the indirect character of the expression will constantly demand renewal and rejuvenation in the form.[36]

For Kierkegaard the openness of thought about life or existence demanded an approach which was unsystematic and abandoned formulas. "Existence" is also something which "constantly demands renewal and rejuvenation in the form." This is one of the things Nietzsche did. He changed the forms with which he approached the issues of life, not in order to conceptualize life but in order to allow it to exist in a variety of its manifestations.

In the question of what philosophy is and where we can get our models, methods and images lie behind this inquiry. To return to Nietzsche:

> We knowers are unknown to ourselves, and for a good reason: how can we ever hope to find what we have never looked for? There is a sound adage which runs: "Where a man's treasure lies, there lies his heart." Our treasure lies in the beehives of our knowledge. We are perpetually on our way thither, being by nature winged insects and honey gatherers of the mind. The only thing that lies close to our heart is the desire to bring something home to the hive. *As for the rest of life—so-called "experience"—who among us is serious enough for that?* Or has time enough? When it comes to such matters, our heart is not in it—we don't even lend our ear.[37]

This and similar passages leave us with the challenge of taking seriously the ideas of life and experience. It is a challenge for us to see how these ideas or images affect Nietzsche's philosophy, and to do this without trivializing or romanticizing them.

Chapter One

FROM METAPHYSICS TO EPISTEMOLOGY TO THE NEW PERSPECTIVE OF PHILOSOPHY

> "Saying Yes to life even in its strangest and hardest problems ...." In this sense I have the right to understand myself as the first tragic philosopher—that is, the most extreme opposite and antipode of a pessimistic philosopher. Before me this transposition of the Dionysian into a philosophical pathos did not exist....[1]

Nietzsche is often seen as an angry and destructive thinker who gives us penetrating moral and social critiques. This credit for his acumen is usually followed by criticism of the entirely unsatisfactory solutions he offers to the problems so skillfully exposed. I would like to correct this view. It is what Nietzsche affirms that I find both interesting and fecund. A careful examination of Nietzsche's critiques is necessary to understand what he recommends, because the positive strategies (both methodological and substantial) are those which are left as live options after others fall or fail in the course of the critique. But destruction is not his aim. My view is that in the course of the destructive and/or deconstructive analysis (especially that which Nietzsche does in his genealogies), a great deal is being affirmed. This is true in terms of what he says about philosophical method and what he offers us substantially as values. We need to follow his stories closely in order to understand what he affirms.

In what follows, some features of his general critical program will be described, beginning with his famous, or infamous, discussion of the death of God. Nietzsche's deeper criticisms of philosophy will then be considered. This examination of the critical writings will extend to his criticisms of conventional moral philosophy and aesthetics. But the analysis will not stop with the destructive portion of his work. Nietzsche's positive program will be considered. The most essential aspect of this is his use of an aesthetic model for the creation of value. This creation extends beyond the aesthetic to all the values which form our relation to life. This relation is examined in the activities which we call moral. The aesthetic model will be used to explain his view of morality and the place of giving value and evaluation in the activity of living.

Nietzsche is perhaps most famous for his penetrating attacks upon Christianity. They form, if not the main source of his influence, at least that of his notoriety. But the aim of Nietzsche's critique is not simply the annihilation of Christian values. With this critique he has attempted to bring about a moral, cultural, and philosophical revolution. He does this by exploring the canonical foundations of Christian values and dogma, and then by attacking these metaphysical underpinnings. The metaphysical presuppositions which bolster the Christian world view go back to the Platonic metaphysical system. In fact, Nietzsche calls Christianity Platonism for the people. It is a simplified version of Platonism with ritual and mystery to please popular tastes.

As we shall see, once Nietzsche succeeds in undermining these foundations many of the values found in society will become suspect. This is because of their historical and theoretical ties with Christian metaphysics. What lay behind this metaphysical system was the Christian God, and all the beliefs and practices which were tied to the existence of that God. Let us look at an example; the "other-worldliness" of the Christian is a part of both Christian and Platonic dogma according to Nietzsche. This "other-worldliness" is the Christian's interest in the world of judgment which is preferred to the world of actual experience. In the Platonic context it is the world of forms or ideas which are also to be preferred to the world of sense. This world is conceived of instead of experienced. Our access to it is by our reason and by detaching the "soul" from the body through a process of intellectual exercises. The Platonic portion of this view has rather obvious ties with Christian doctrine as well. The world of the Christian God, and the model of perfect knowledge the God is supposed to possess, follow along the lines of the Platonic metaphysic as well. This metaphysic still has a hold on those of us who live in largely Christian cultures. It is so much a part of the way we see the world that we do not think about it. It becomes invisible because it is a piece of accepted dogma.

> Very few manage to see a problem in that which makes our daily life, that to which we have long since grown accustomed —our eyes are not adjusted to it: this seems to me to be the case especially in regard to our morality.[2]

Nietzsche is concerned with making visible some of the things we have taken for granted, hence to expose these beliefs to critical thought and possibly to reform.

If the other-worldliness mentioned above is subjected to a critique, then it is made visible. When this happens, the possibility of other explanations for the Christian's world view can be entertained. Nietzsche does just this. He criticizes some aspects of the view, as we shall see below, and then offers a social historical account of how the belief in another world arose. He suggests that we substitute this story for the metaphysical explanations which were a part of the established dogma. These were believed to follow from the Christian God's existence. Nietzsche finds that tied to the belief in another world is a spirit of rancor and a desire for vengeance. According to him the Christians wanted vengeance for the wrongs they had to suffer in their slavish condition. Since these wrongs were obviously not righted in this world, the Jews (early Christians) projected on the heavens a world where they were righted and a time, in the not too distant future (the second coming was originally expected during the lives of the apostles), when vengeance would be wreaked on those who oppressed them in this world.

Lest we think that Nietzsche, the nihilist or pessimist, merely postulates this reprehensible idea and attributes it to the Christians, we are given evidence. He quotes the saints and "Fathers" of the church. Thomas Aquinas says, "The blessed in the kingdom of heaven will see the punishments of the damned '*in order that their bliss will be more delightful for them*'"[3] and Quintus Septimus

Florens Tertullian tells us:

> ... But think what awaits us on the day of his [Christ's] triumph! ... *What sight shall wake my wonder, what my laughter, what my joy and exultation* as I see all those kings ... groaning in the depths of darkness! ... And the magistrates who persecuted the name of Jesus, liquefying in fiercer flames than they kindled in their rage against the Christians! Those sages too, the philosophers blushing before their disciples as they blaze together, ...[4]

It may be that this religion, ostensibly founded on love and forgiveness, begins to lose its hold on us when we uncover the rancorous motives behind early Christian metaphysical beliefs.

The end Nietzsche has in mind is not that we simply condemn Christianity. In fact, it may be that the preoccupation with passing judgment is itself a Christian vice. The idea that Christian metaphysics encourages us to think in terms of making judgments will be explored in more depth in the following two chapters. Nietzsche prefers to allow and encourage re-evaluation. We must look carefully into the origins of practices we wish to evaluate.

Obscuring origins is a conservative device. By obscuring origins we ward off criticism, and, hence, prevent change. In this case, since the phenomenon claims to have a transcendental origin, obscuring the origins leaves the thinker or practitioners with the impression that it is not in our power to change. This impression may remain even if we realize that it is in our power to question. In this case, if we do not believe that the belief in another world arose in time, we are encouraged to believe that it will not end in time. It began, according to its champions, instead with the will of a god. This god is a being over whom we have little or no control. To show a worldly origin to the practices and beliefs, and to show a time when they did not exist, is an enormous help in allowing these beliefs to loosen their hold upon us.

The re-evaluation of all values which Nietzsche speaks of will involve a new consideration of these old values. It will require a purging of those values which have no justification apart from that found in the Christian metaphysics. We do not simply throw the old values out, we consider whether they are worth reinvesting with value and meaning.

The re-evaluation is part of both Nietzsche's positive and negative programs. It is part of the negative or destructive project because it completes the critique which Nietzsche has begun. It does this by rooting out all the beliefs and practices which rested on the now questionable metaphysic and subjecting them to scrutiny. But it is also part of the positive program in that once we have done this, in fact, while we are doing it, we can begin to re-value and create values. Nietzsche is not overthrowing Christian values in order to leave us with nothing. We are building our values in doing the critique. We are re-valuing some old values, de-valuing some, and creating others which become our criteria during the process. This language, the "valuing of values," may seem strange, but for Nietzsche a value is something which is willed or created. So all valuing is an activity which shows our beliefs, prejudices, and desires. We show the way we value different values by acting on them. We re-evaluate them in the course of living. For Nietzsche the valuing is shown in both our beliefs and actions. In this he differs from Jean-Paul Sartre, who believes that we find our values and their worth primarily in what we achieve and do. For both of these thinkers a value is not something which is given (by god, for example) or found (for example, in nature).

At least a tentative value is implied in this scrutiny. Values are more fundamental or necessary for knowledge than as the criteria of our success because, without values, we cannot even begin the process.

> The question of values is more *fundamental* than the question of certainty: the latter becomes serious only by pre-supposing that the value question has already been answered.[5]

In order to scrutinize a value, we need a viewpoint. We need something in which we believe or have "faith."

> Strictly speaking, there is no such thing as science "without any presuppositions"; this thought does not bear thinking through, it is paralogical: a philosophy, a "faith," must always be there first of all, so that science can acquire from it a direction, a meaning, a limit, a method, a *right* to exist....[6]

For Nietzsche, all activity whether it be moral or epistemological is value laden. The "values" are the presuppositions of our thought. They are believed or willed. The questions then arise, not over whether or not something is a value, but, between values. Even logic, even matters which seem to have to do with method instead of facts or assertions, are not immune to Nietzsche's propensity to find values hiding everywhere.

> But *logical* evaluations are not the deepest or most fundamental to which our audacious mistrust can descend: faith in reason, with which the validity of these judgments must stand or fall, is, as faith, a *moral* phenomenon ....[7]

Logic and reason are themselves both things which are retained and sustained by an act of will or by belief. There are no givens, neither metaphysically (as in Platonic or Christian forms) nor psychologically and epistemologically (as Immanuel Kant would prefer).

The process of re-evaluation is not as neat as we might like because of the nature of the revolutionary activity. But according to Nietzsche we are not dealing with the simple substitution of one dogma for another and, as a result, tentative values must be raised and tried. The process cannot be fitted into a formula.

The easiest and quickest way to review Nietzsche's critique of philosophy is by considering his metaphor of the death of God. Nietzsche asks us to accept the death of God on hypothesis so that we can see what follows from it. He does not argue for it as a thesis. In the works we will be looking at, he simply alludes to the "death" as a cultural phenomenon. It is the consequences of the death of God which interest Nietzsche, not the establishment of the fact. Nietzsche talks about the consequence of God's demise in the following passage from *The Gay Science:*

> After Buddha was dead, his shadow was still shown for centuries in a cave—a tremendous, gruesome shadow. God is dead; but given the way of men, there may still be caves for thousands of years in which his shadow will be shown.—And we—we still have to vanquish his shadow, too.[8]

God is dead, and yet in another form lives on. We have stopped believing in God but what of the values, traditions, and other assumptions which rested upon this belief? Are they not now suspect? Consider the extent of the influence of the shadow of God. Religious rituals and observations include festivals, celebrations, and days of atonement. Sanctioned practices surround birth, marriage, and death. A whole variety of less ritualized customs and superstitions have grown up around the canonical practice. In effect, an entire ethical system surrounds us, including a set of rules and the enforcement of those rules through the threat of retribution (hell) and the pressure to communal conformity (the inquisition is merely an extreme form of this).

Note the extent of what Nietzsche considers to be moral or morally relevant. Nietzsche does not merely concern himself with the more familiar moral rules, like the prohibitions against murder and incest, but also the customs and mores of the people. In fact, in some ways these less visible, less "significant," values and practices are of more importance. This is true for the reasons mentioned above. Customs and mores have not been given much attention, and yet have a greater hold over our lives. This is precisely because they are not examined, not questioned.

With the death of God we find that all of these values and practices are without a foundation. Nietzsche continues this theme in the passage called "The Madman."[9] But now Nietzsche uses an even more vivid image. The Madman tries to point out to those around him, many of whom already consider themselves to be atheists, what they have done by killing God. He asks them, "Do we smell nothing yet of God's decomposition? Gods too decompose." What is this divine decomposition? It is the general wasting away of all those values and practices which had their sole justification in the life, in the existence of God. What the atheists have failed to realize is the extent to which many practices in their lives still revolve around "Christian" beliefs. The Madman's action could have another meaning. He may say his mass to ensure that this God does not return. Perhaps it is better that he stays where he is in eternal repose, and out of the affairs of human beings. In this way we can continue to develop our concern with this world without interference. This interpretation suggested itself when thinking about Dostoyevsky's chapter from *The Brothers Karamazov* called the "Grand Inquisitor." In it the Cardinal attempts to ensure that Jesus doesn't interfere with his worldly work. The idea that Dostoyevsky influenced Nietzsche is an anachronistic interpretation, if taken literally. Nietzsche did not read Dostoyevsky until early 1887 or late 1886 at the earliest and he does not, to my knowledge, ever mention reading *The Brothers Karamazov.* This book also contains an interesting literary example of "divine" decomposition. It can be found in the character Father Zossima in *The Brothers Karamazov.* At his death this unusually "pure" man decomposes with a vengeance.

When the Madman entered the market place he claimed to search for God. He was taken as insane and ridiculed, partially, because some of those around him were atheists. They teased him about this God. He carried a lantern in "the bright morning hours" as one who has lost both his way and his sense of what is appropriate. Yet he explains, "Do we not need to light lanterns in the morning?" Now that we have lost our direction, lost the meaning of our life, lost the light which guided us (God). The townspeople first take the Madman as coming on a ridiculous quest: the search for God. But we soon see that it is not God for whom the Madman is searching. Instead the Madman has a message and a prophecy. The message reminds the people around him of the extent to which belief in God has affected their life, and hence how directionless and purposeless their lives will become unless they give themselves direction. The prophecy regards the consequences of this deed, of the murder of God:

> Must we not become Gods simply to be worthy of it [killing God]? There has never been a greater deed; and whoever is born after us—for the sake of this deed he will belong to a higher history than all history hitherto.

We must take upon ourselves the responsibility for the values in society. We can no longer pretend to defer to a higher power, no longer turn our eyes from this world to another. Taking responsibility, in this context, is not meant to conjure up a notion of responsibility which is commonly associated with guilt, especially not one which relates to culpability and passing judgment. To Nietzsche that would be no progress—only another leaden idea to weigh our reason and life down. Again the "Christian" preoccupation with judgment and the perspective of the judge (and God) would come to the fore. (This will be further discussed in the following sections.) What responsibility does mean is that we acknowledge the authorship of our values as individual and cultural creations.

But the madman, in the end, is not heeded. He says:

> I have come too early ... deeds, though done, still require time to be seen and heard. This deed is still more distant from them than the most distant stars—*and yet they have done it themselves*.

The madman then goes into various churches and conducts his own mass for the eternal repose of God's soul. It seems that he is the only one who mourns because he alone knows what he has "lost." He explains that the churches are now nothing more than "the tombs and sepulchers of God." Although they are this there is as yet no other place to mourn and so his action has a strange and poignant irony.

There is no reason to doubt that Nietzsche believes that God is dead. This is not something he argues for; it is simply something which he observes and assumes. The extent of God's meaningfulness in our lives has atrophied since its height in the middle ages. God has gone from being the author of creation, the source for meaning in human existence, the principle of explanation in the natural world, and the source of legal and moral legislation; to being merely the enforcer of private morality and the keeper of religious ritual, and in many cases not even this.

Nietzsche obviously does not want us to go back to the belief in God. What we should do is be creative and intelligent atheists. To do this, we must actively inquire into the extent to which the belief in God and Christian metaphysics has permeated Western society. Many people who do not believe in God go along complacently as non-believers, and yet remain engaged in the vestigial practices of religion, continuing to affirm values which had their sole justification in Judeo-Christian metaphysics. This is wrong and senseless.

In *Daybreak*, §149, published in 1881, Nietzsche talks of "the need for little deviant acts."[10] It is necessary that we note the extended sense of what constitutes morality which is implied in this passage. Nietzsche is giving an example of what many "tolerably free-minded people" do. As we saw in the Madman passage, even the people who had freed themselves from some "Christian" beliefs did not always realize the more subtle consequences of what they were doing. In the following passage we see that Nietzsche is giving us some examples of how necessary it is to carry out the consequences of our beliefs in the "little" everyday actions of our lives.

> Sometimes to act *against* our better judgment when it comes to questions of *custom;* to give way in practice while keeping our reservations to ourselves, to do as everyone does and thus show them consideration as though in compensation for our deviant opinions:—many tolerably free-minded people regard this, not merely as unobjectionable, but as "honest," "humane," "tolerant," "not being pedantic," and whatever else those pretty words may be with which the intellectual conscience is lulled to sleep .... "It doesn't *really matter* if people like us also do what everyone else does and always has done"—this is the thoughtless *prejudice!* The *thoughtless* error! For nothing *matters more* than that an already mighty, anciently established and irrationally recognised custom should be once more confirmed by a person recognised as rational: it thereby acquires in the eyes of all who come to

> hear of it the sanction of rationality itself! All respect to your opinions! But *little deviant acts* are worth more!

Sometimes, even if we have radical opinions, we go along with customs almost as an apology for the radicalness of our ideas:

> ... and thus [for example] this person takes his child for Christian baptism though he is an atheist; and that person serves in the army as all the world does, however much he may execrate hatred between nations; and a third marries his wife in church because her relatives are pious and is not ashamed to repeat vows before a priest.

To Nietzsche it is precisely these little deviant acts, the practices which instance our belief, which matter:

> For nothing *matters more* than that an already mighty, anciently established and irrationally recognized custom should be once more confirmed by a person recognized rational: it thereby acquires in the eyes of all who come to hear of it the sanction of rationality itself.

As a consequence of this, it is our business to stop affirming those customs, even those which seem insignificant, even if our motivation is to make life easier or "better" for someone else. Altruism is no excuse.

I have called the death of God a metaphor. It is a metaphor because its purpose is to give us a quite concrete image of what it feels like to abandon a transcendental perspective. One of the problems with the transcendental perspective found in the case of God is that it is perceived, or worse conceived, instead of lived. Its greatest danger lies in this fact.

> The concept of "God" invented as a counterconcept of life—everything harmful, poisonous, slanderous, the whole hostility unto death against life synthesized in this concept in a gruesome unity! The concept of the "beyond," the "true world" invented in order to devaluate the only world there is—in order to retain no goal, no reason, no task for our earthly reality! The concept of the "soul," the "Spirit," finally even "immortal soul," invented in order to despise the body, to make it sick, "holy"; to oppose with a ghastly levity everything that deserves to be taken seriously in life, the questions of nourishment, abode, spiritual diet, treatment of the sick, cleanliness, and weather.[11]

This turning back to life in the concrete reality of our experience of it (as seen in the above quotation) is really Nietzsche's main concern: to turn us back to life and living as positive values. To teach us to affirm all aspects of life, the painful with the joyous. We should not give up the joy in life for the sake of concentration on the sorrow, nor should we ignore the real pain and suffering for a vision which denies them. We should be able to embrace them both and will the continuation of our life. If we can do this, then we are well disposed to life: this is the test of morality.

Our disposition toward life is the lesson of the passage in *The Gay Science*, §341, called "the Greatest Weight." In this passage the possibility of an eternity which is not other-worldly is entertained. This is one which would cause us to look at our lives as we live them and judge their value ourselves. We would judge them as the ultimate value, because they would be eternity: the eternal repetition of the same. Nietzsche manages to get us to take worldly values seriously and to be our own judges by employing a "Christian" or other-worldly device (it is actually an idea found in antiquity), the idea of another world. Although this time the other world is identical to the one of our life.

He asks what if eternity simply is life, as we now live it.—Only not just life once; to be lived through and forgotten, but life repeated with every detail to all eternity. The demon says:

> "This life as you now live it, and have lived it, you will have to live once more and innumerable times more; and there will be nothing new in it, but every pain and every joy and every thought and sigh and everything unutterably small or great in your life will have to return to you, all in the same succession and sequence ...."[12]

The test of morality then would be a question of how well you lived with yourself, and how you lived with the things you could control and those which you could not. Nietzsche ends this experiment by asking "Or how well disposed would you have to become to yourself and to life *to crave nothing more fervently* than this ultimate eternal confirmation and seal?"—To not only be able to tolerate this idea of eternity, but to be able to embrace it, is to say "Yes" to life.—Not some rarefied form of life, not some aspects and not others, but actual life, all of it: your life.

What we have considered so far should give us some perspective on Nietzsche's supposed nihilism and the fact that he is often taken to be merely a destructive thinker. His so-called "nihilism" has often simply meant his negation of Christian values. If these were taken by critics to be the only real values, then Nietzsche's criticism meant for them the negation of all values. Or for others who are not Christian (post-Christian?) but yet retain the understanding of values as given instead of created or as having a concrete nature (by virtue of their attachment to reason, for example), a similar criticism might arise. Nietzsche is considered a pessimist because he does not acknowledge the possibility of their type of value and especially because he finds their search and desire for such values atavistic and "Christian." Something which they believe they have gone beyond. This was the case with the atheists mentioned in the

"Madman" section. They did not understand the purpose of the Madman's visit any more than the others. They assumed that since they were atheists they were well beyond anything which the Madman could say to them. Instead they merely fail to understand the message: he had come too early.

Nietzsche also turns the tables on those who would call him a nihilist or pessimist, by making the accusation first. In his work, as we shall see, it is the Christians and positivists who are labeled the pessimists. The Christians negate the reality of the lived world, the world of becoming, for the sake of a conceived world; one which Nietzsche believes is motivated, at least in part, by a desire for revenge. The positivists are likewise guilty of a distortion which has its basis in pessimism. They distort the world as perceived into a world containing regularities which give them the illusion of control over it. We will examine this case in more detail later in this chapter. According to Nietzsche, part of the superiority of earlier Greek views of the moral world (as represented in drama, for example) is that there is an acknowledgment of the fact that part of our fate is out of our hands. In early Greek culture this was both a strength and a weakness. There was an excess of pessimism which endangered that culture.[13] In many ways Nietzsche's critique of Western culture is like Heinrich Heine's. Heine too considers both Greeks and Christians pessimists. Heine also speaks of the gods as fellow inhabitants of a universe instead of as sacred beings apart. But Heine is still engaged with them, engaged with a passion, while for Nietzsche they are no longer real: they were there for a purpose and the purpose is now largely symbolic. We can see this in the case of the legend of Buddha mentioned above.

What Nietzsche says about the Christian God has another purpose, and that purpose is to give us an image of our "real" relation to the world. That relation is our connection to it by means of our bodies, culture, history, and life experiences. We have seen this alluded to in *Ecce Homo*, "Why I am a destiny," §8. When we do not have the example of this God's omniscient eye we must perforce come crashing down to earth. This is precisely what Nietzsche wants. And when we do, we must acknowledge in this world and in our "distorted" perspective of it, the interest and business of the new philosophers, "the philosophers of tragic knowledge."

These philosophers do not abandon God and metaphysics with a skeptical and malicious joy (although Nietzsche himself has often been accused of being so motivated and indeed often does seem to take a kind of perverse satisfaction in dismantling some "truth"). They, like the Madman, realize the depth and extent of their "loss." This is true even if what is lost is only another creative illusion.

> *The philosopher of tragic knowledge. He* masters the uncontrolled knowledge drive, though not by means of a new metaphysics. He establishes no new faith. He considers it *tragic* that the ground of metaphysics has been withdrawn, and he will never permit himself to be satisfied with the motley whirling game of the sciences. He cultivates a new *life*; he returns to art its rights.

> The philosopher of *desperate knowledge* will be absorbed in blind science: knowledge at any price. For the tragic philosopher the appearance of the metaphysical as merely anthropomorphic completes the *picture of existence.*
> He is not a *skeptic.*
> Here there is a concept which must be *created*, for skepticism is not the goal. When carried to its limits the knowledge drive turns against itself in order to proceed to the *critique of knowing.* Knowledge in the service of the best life. One must even *will illusion*—that is what is tragic.[14]

Tragic though the "loss" is, it invites us into another way of knowing and being. As we see above, the model is aesthetic and creative (but we will return to this). Nietzsche considered himself to be a tragic philosopher.[15] He wants to make it clear that a great deal has been "lost." The fact that what is lost is illusory makes it no less of a loss. Nietzsche's point is that the tragic philosopher is one who, like the Madman, realizes the extent of the loss. This philosopher realizes that the whole project of philosophy must be modified. It is not enough to establish a new faith to replace the old one. This is what the positivists do (as we shall see below). They are the philosophers of desperate knowledge.[16] They are still engaged in trying to achieve certainty. They haven't abandoned the old conception of knowledge, which is something we can capture (*Beyond Good and Evil*, Preface). This quotation also introduces, fairly early in Nietzsche's career, the fact that Nietzsche does not feel the impossibility of a certain kind of knowledge will leave us with skepticism and pessimism.

With the philosopher of tragic knowledge Nietzsche returns to what he takes to be a Greek notion of philosophy in general, and epistemology in particular. The idea is that all knowing does or should serve life. The Greeks show their understanding of this by demanding that all thought be immediately translatable into action. Thought and action make up a unity.

> The Greeks themselves, possessed of an inherently insatiable thirst for knowledge, controlled it by their ideal need for and consideration of all the values of life. Whatever they learned, they wanted to live through, immediately.[17]

Nietzsche goes on to say that a search for knowledge can barbarize and that the Greeks escaped this by keeping knowledge and truth involved in the activity of living. This practice he opposes to contemporary philosophy and "our drive toward truth ... which asks merely 'And what is life worth, after all?'"[18]

> The Greeks ... knew how to *learn:* an immense power of appropriation. Our age should not think that it stands so much higher in terms of its knowledge drive—except that in the case of the Greeks everything was *life*!
> With us it remains knowledge![19]

We will have to return to this notion of life and consider how creative illusions will replace metaphysics just as the notion of perspectival knowing transforms the traditional epistemology.

As a metaphor the death of God signals not only the collapse of those values, explanations, and practices which were dependent upon the Judeo-Christian God for their legitimacy, but also the more encompassing collapse of metaphysics. Rhetorically this works quite nicely for Nietzsche. As I have suggested, this God is the perfect symbol for the transcendental point of view. The God has the perspective which is perspectiveless. It sees everything from every possible perspective or from outside a perspective; in short, it has perfect knowledge. It creates and justifies absolute values which lie outside of time because they repose in the breast of an eternal God. It creates and sustains the laws which govern the universe and thus guarantees their reliability and necessity.

It is customary, when considering Nietzsche's work, to view the death of God as having primarily moral and religious significance. I think that we must take our interpretation beyond this. Nietzsche is not just questioning Christianity, he is criticizing the way philosophy is done. He is interested in the overthrow of metaphysics, but his critique goes much further, and includes all transcendental and even positivist philosophy. We have already had a glimpse of this in the example of the philosopher of desperate knowledge. In *The Gay Science*, §347, "Believers and their need to believe," he writes:

> Christianity, it seems to me, is still needed by most people in old Europe even today; therefore it still finds believers .... Metaphysics is still needed by some; but so is that impetuous *demand for certainty* that today discharges itself among large numbers of people in a scientific-positivistic form. The demand that one *wants* by all means that something should be firm (while on account of the ardor of this demand one is easier and more negligent about the demonstration of this certainty)—this, too, is still the demand for a support, a prop, in short that *instinct of weakness* which, to be sure, does not create religious, metaphysical systems, and convictions of all kinds but—conserves them.[20]

Nietzsche seems to think that Christianity has sustained our belief in and desire for these transcendental explanations. Christianity legitimated the desire by giving us the example which justified the possibility: God already knew. In this way we could try to attain God's perspective. Some of these desires have remained and affected positive science. "Residues of Christian value judgments are found everywhere in socialistic and positivistic systems. A *critique of Christian morality* is still lacking."[21]

It is Christian morality and all that supports it which allow us to continue projects which deny our own interested and involved perspective. The fact that we can still think of our projects, for example, those of positive science, as neutral or disinterested shows the extent to which we have failed to reexamine and root out all that was tied to these systems. One has only to consider the extent of the Cartesian skepticism to realize how trusting and ready to believe Descartes actually was. In spite of his "radical" doubt he quickly accepted whatever would justify his conservative system. This is evident both in his faith in the simple and in the "discovery" of a method for finding truth by using the clarity and distinctness criterion. Consider how conservative his doubt seems to us today. He does not question the workings or meanings of the language he uses, nor the transparency of the self to the self.

> ***How we, too, are still pious.***— In science (Wissenschaft), convictions have no rights of citizenship, as we say with good reason. Only when they decide to descend to the modesty of hypotheses, of a provisional experimental point of view, of a regulative fiction, they may be granted admission and even a certain value in the realm of knowledge—though always with the restriction that they remain under police supervision under the police of mistrust. —But does this not mean, if you consider it more precisely, that a conviction may obtain admission to science only when it *ceases to* be a conviction? Would it not be the first step in the discipline of the scientific spirit that we would not permit ourselves any more convictions?
>
> Probably this is so; only we still have to ask: *To make it possible for this discipline to begin*, must there not be some prior conviction—even one that is so commanding and unconditional that it sacrifices all other convictions to itself? We see that science also rests on a faith; there simply is no science "without presuppositions." The question whether *truth* is needed must not only have been affirmed in advance, but affirmed to such a degree that the principle, the faith, the conviction finds expression: "*Nothing* is needed *more* than truth, and in relation to it everything else has only second-rate value...."

This is to a large extent a reiteration of the point we looked at earlier in the section from *On The Genealogy of Morals*. The quotation continues:

> Thus the question "Why science?" leads back to the moral problem: *Why have morality at all* when life, nature, and history are "not moral"? No doubt, those who are truthful in that audacious and ultimate sense that is presupposed by the faith in science *thus affirm another world* than the world of life, nature, and history; and insofar as they affirm this "other world"—look, must they not by the same token negate its counterpart, this world, *our* world?—But you will have gathered what I am driving at, namely, that it is still a

> *metaphysical faith* upon which our faith in science rests—that even we seekers after knowledge today, we godless anti-metaphysicians still take our fire, too, from the flame lit by a faith that is thousands of years old, that Christian faith which was also the faith of Plato, that God is the truth, that truth is divine.—But what if this should become more and more incredible, if nothing should prove to be divine any more unless it were error, blindness, the lie—if God himself should prove to be our most enduring lie?[22]

The way we look at life and being, our view of truth, and the very methods by which we approach knowledge are tainted by this life-negating remainder, this "faith" of Christian metaphysics.

As we have said, with the death of God we have a vivid image or picture of the consequences of giving up the transcendental perspective. The focus of Christianity is on another world, the world of God who has the perspective of a creator and the world of eternity, the world after judgment. This world, the world of our life, is, in the latter case, seen as a trial which will determine an individual's lot in the real world to come. In it, we human beings have only part of the picture. We are bound to earth and to the perspective and the life of an inhabitant, one from which we cannot see all things, cannot know the future, cannot unravel the mysteries behind the behavior of nature. Yet the answer to the human question is promised for the believer if he or she will only wait. In other words, an answer is presumed to exist although it is not yet known. It is assumed that there is an answer and a being who has it, but this answer is not and will not be revealed in this life.

As a consequence of this world view, the world of our life and experience is denigrated, but also because of it our beliefs about the nature of this world are distorted. Instead of seeing the world as it appears to us while we live, we try to adopt the perspective which we know is possible because it is actual, namely God's. We then think of ways we might legitimate that quest. For example: we think that we are created in God's image and that we have the reason of God, although not so powerful. So perhaps we can imagine a transcendental point of view or achieve it, especially if we leave behind the part of us which is so necessarily, or rather obviously, tied to this earth: our bodies and our senses. Why these are not seen as also divine or in God's image is not clear except that it is established by Pauline doctrine[23] and to question it in most forms of Christianity amounts to heresy. This "leaving behind" begins as a spiritual quest of the saints and martyrs. It continues in the work, rather than activity, of the saints become philosophers for example, in the work of Aquinas.

Eventually this desire for detachment will be continued in the work of the Protestant philosopher Kant. It appears in his work in a more disguised form. It is interesting to note that we do not often refer to Kant as a religious thinker. Perhaps this is precisely because of the reasons which Nietzsche gave: that Kant is careful to obscure the origins and motivations of his thought. "In the case of Kant, theological prejudice, his unconscious dogmatism, his moralistic perspective, were dominant, directing, commanding."[24] Nietzsche enjoys unmasking Kant's other motivations as well.

> ... to create room for *his* "moral realm" he (Kant) saw himself obliged to posit an undemonstrable world, a logical "Beyond"—it was for precisely that that he had need of his critique of pure reason! In other words: *he would never have had need of it* if one thing had not been more vital to him than anything else: to render the "moral realm" unassailable, even better incomprehensible to reason—for he felt that a moral order of things was only too assailable by reason! In the face of nature and history, in face of the thorough *immorality* of nature and history, Kant was, like every good German of the old stamp, a pessimist; he believed in morality, not because it is demonstrated in nature and history, but in spite of the fact that nature and history continually contradict it.[25]

So Kant's world view, although it avoids the obvious metaphysical presuppositions and dogmas, still has behind it an attempt to go beyond the world of experience. Again Kant's very methodology, his "critique" is made necessary by the values or world which he was trying to preserve in the "moral realm." Behind Kant's thought and critiques lay disguised "convictions." The fact that convictions exist is not in itself a problem. However, the fact that they are disguised (and assumed to be absent), and that they are the "wrong" ones, is a problem.

Because this God is seen as the author of creation and because God is intelligent and purposeful, the world is believed to have a structure and to be intelligible—at least to God. As a result, the world is looked at as having a purposive or organic structure. Nietzsche attempts to get us to abandon these teleological explanations of nature and he questions the presumption of order in the universe. He says further: "Let us even beware of believing that the universe is a machine: it is certainly not constructed for one purpose, and calling it a 'machine' does it far too much honor."[26]

> The total character of the world, however, is in all eternity chaos—in the sense not of a lack of necessity but of a lack of order, arrangement, form, beauty, wisdom, and whatever other names there are for our aesthetic anthropomorphisms .... Let us beware of attributing to it [the universe] heartlessness and unreason or their opposites: it is neither perfect nor beautiful, nor noble, nor does it wish to become any of these things; it does not by any means strive to imitate man .... Let us beware of saying there are laws in nature. There are only necessities.... Once you know that there are no purposes, you also know that there is no accident; for it is only beside a world of purposes that the word "accident" has any meaning....

> When will all these shadows of God cease to darken our minds? When will we complete our de-deification of nature? When may we begin to "*naturalize*" humanity in terms of a pure, newly discovered, newly redeemed nature?[27]

Again Nietzsche is trying to force us, to cajole us, away from this God and all it represents in regard to the way we view the world and ourselves. From our vantage point in this world, hurled back to earth, we must realize that we necessarily see things from a perspective and from a situation. In a sense Nietzsche is a conventional post Kantian thinker: the issues are for him epistemological instead of metaphysical. The vital questions involve the way we are tied to the world by our understanding, but the question of knowledge or knowing must not be construed in the narrow sense commonly found in the discipline. Nietzsche wants to consider the context of knowing and place the activity in a thinking, living being. He emphasized the sensual character of our involvement in the world as well as the social and cultural context. All of these factors influence us as knowers.

The notion of knowledge and truth that he is criticizing here is part of that "demand for certainty" which was discussed above.[28] This is a notion of truth which he sees as lying behind the Christian, metaphysical, and even positivist accounts which he is criticizing. It suggests a view of the world as static, and hence underemphasizes things necessary to human endeavors which fail to have this characteristic. This move, which can be seen as coming back to earth from the heavens or down to earth from the over-reliance on abstract principles of explanation, is one which Nietzsche is trying to compel us to make throughout his writings and in a variety of ways. We must give up the search for a way out of what is so obviously our situation in the world. Instead we need to look at that situation in new ways.

Nietzsche is anxious to tie together his critiques of traditional epistemology and metaphysics. It is easier to see these connections when we see his points within the context of the history of philosophy. He does this in a number of places. We find it in his writings about ancient Greek philosophy, which we will explore in his writings from *Philosophy in the Tragic Age of the Greeks;* and in those which deal with the history that leads us to contemporary philosophy, as in the idea of a "true" world, found in the *Twilight of the Idols*. It is time to go beyond the critique of Christianity, which is, after all, only part of the story, to look at these issues in a more strictly philosophical context; also, to look at what is a proper philosophical context.

Nietzsche explores the changes in the conceptions of philosophy and its birth in a variety of historical contexts. The following passages are primarily from his history of philosophy in ancient Greece: *Philosophy in the Tragic Age of the Greeks*. This is an early work written 1870-1873 but not published in his lifetime. In the first passage we have Nietzsche's interpretation of the situation in which these early Greek philosophers found themselves.

> The Greeks, among whom Thales stood out so suddenly, were

> the very opposite of realists, in that they believed only in the reality of men and gods, looking upon all of nature as but a disguise, a masquerade, or a metamorphosis of these god-men. Man for them was the truth and the core of all things; everything else was but semblance and the play of illusion. For this very reason they found it unbelievably difficult to comprehend concepts as such. Herein they were the exact opposite of modern man. For us, even the most personal is sublimated into abstraction; for them, the greatest abstraction kept running back into a person.[29]

The difference in Thales's work is his interest in abstractions and conceptualizations. This separates him and his philosophy from the mythology which has come before.

> ... the thought of Thales ... has its value precisely in the fact that it was meant non-mythically and non-allegorically .... Man for them [the Greeks] was the truth and the core of all things; everything else was but semblance and the play of illusion.[30]

The case of Thales is different because mathematics and astronomy form a paradigm for his work and for his ideas about truth. Thales's work stands out as "philosophical" against a background of belief in mythical worlds. Nietzsche doesn't find the work's value in the ontological unity of his principle of explanation (that everything is water), but rather in the new ideas of confirmation and truth borrowed from the above mentioned discipline, but here applied to the world of human life as well.

In the work of Heraclitus, a later thinker, the value is on the ever-changing elements which make up living. One element of this is his conception of time, which is fluid. This conception of time is based on the way time is lived and felt. It is not based on an abstraction formed from an intellectualized notion of time. To understand time we do not go outside of our experience of it; instead, we consider the ever changing fluctuations which make up the way it feels to us.

> As Heraclitus sees time, so does Schopenhauer. He repeatedly said of it that every moment in it exists only insofar as it has just consumed the preceding one, its father, and is then immediately consumed likewise. And that past and future are as perishable as any dream, but that the present is but the dimensionless and durationless borderline between the two. And that space is just like time ... [relativity of these notions] .... This is a truth of the greatest immediate self-evidence for everyone, and one which for this very reason is extremely difficult to reach by way of concept or reason.[31]

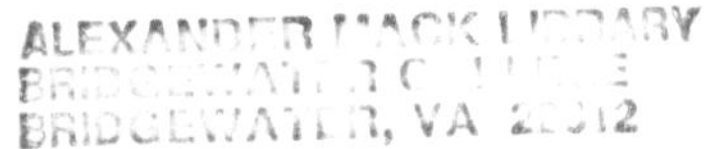
ALEXANDER MACK LIBRARY
BRIDGEWATER, VA

Heraclitus's "self-evidence," in this case, is based upon reference to experience. The understanding of time should be intuitively plausible; it should accord with what we feel and see. The proof for such "knowing" is rhetorical instead of logical. An appeal is made from knower to knower, an appeal to look at each of their perceptions of time and see whether it corresponds with that of the other. Just as presuppositions were seen to be "paralogical," so too is this knowledge.

Instead of seeing in the world lawfulness or control, Heraclitus was interested in the dynamic quality which informs all aspects of the world. It is for this reason that Nietzsche admired his work above that of all other Greek thinkers. He speaks of "... Heraclitus, in whose proximity I feel altogether warmer and better than anywhere else."[32]

> What he [Heraclitus] saw, the teaching of *law in becoming* and of *play in necessity*, must be seen from now on in all eternity. He raised the curtain on this greatest of all dramas.[33]

Heraclitus has a notion of life, and of the play of forces, which is attractive to Nietzsche. He neither reduces the world to a single material substance, nor to a timeless structure. The strife, conflict, and interaction of his world must take place in time. That time, as we have seen above, is a time whose rhythm (measure and flow) is that of lived experience.

In contrast to this view is the work of Parmenides, where the interest was to obscure the multiplicity and ever-changing quality of life. Nietzsche is critical of both Parmenides's conclusions and his methodology and goals.

> What astonishes us [in Parmenides] is the degree of schematism and abstraction (in a Greek!), above all, the terrible energetic striving for *certainty* in an epoch which otherwise thought mythically and whose imagination was highly mobile and fluid.[34]

This is another example of what Nietzsche thinks is the wrong-headed goal of epistemology: certainty.

Parmenides's ontology gives us a world which is static, one in which multiplicity has given way to unity. This is true in spite of the fact that:

> Experience nowhere offered him being as he imagined it, but he concluded its existence from the fact that he was able to think it. This is a conclusion which rests on the assumption that we have an organ of knowledge which reaches into the essence of things and is independent of experience.[35]

This is the beginning of a belief which Nietzsche believes has been quite harmful. The belief in reason or some power which when disassociated from experience claims to achieve truth and certainty. Nietzsche goes on to say, in criticism of such a view:

> Now Aristotle asserted against a similar reasoning that that existence is never an intrinsic part of essence. One may never infer the *existentia* of being from the concept being—whose *essentia* is nothing more than being itself.

This is, unfortunately, the beginning of belief in the other worldliness or rather non-worldliness which Nietzsche is still fighting against. Parmenides's break with Heraclitus is evident in his preference for the idea of being over becoming. Nietzsche continues his criticism of Parmenides: "The concept of being! As though it did not show its low empirical origin in its very etymology! For *esse* basically means 'to breathe.'"[36] It is from the world in which we live that we derive the concept of being at all (if Nietzsche's etymology is correct).

In the work of these early philosophers we begin to see the "philosopher's traits" which Nietzsche criticizes in the *Twilight of the Idols*, III §1. These are: "their lack of a historical sense, their hatred of the very idea of becoming."[37] He continues, "They think that they show their *respect* for a subject when they de-historicize it, *sub specie aeterni* ...."[38] It is precisely the taking things out of their context which makes them less well known, according to Nietzsche.

In order to better understand Nietzsche's criticisms of philosophy, it is, also, worth looking at what might be the most concise history of Western theories of reality (with commentary!). These are the passages in the *Twilight of the Idols*, "How the 'True World' finally became a fable."

> 1. The History of an Error
>
> 1. The true world—attainable for the sage, the pious, the virtuous man; he lives in it, *he is it.* (The oldest form of the idea, relatively sensible, simple, and persuasive. A circumlocution for the sentence "I, Plato, *am* the truth.")
> 2. The true world—unattainable for now, but promised for the sage, the pious, the virtuous man ("for the sinner who repents"). (Progress of an idea: it becomes more subtle, insidious, incomprehensible—*it becomes female*, it becomes Christian).
> 3. The true world—unattainable, indemonstrable, unpromisable; but the very thought of it—a consolation, an obligation, an imperative. (At bottom, the old sun, but seen through mist and skepticism. The idea has become elusive, pale, Nordic, Königsbergian).
> 4. The true world—unattainable? At any rate, unattained. And being unattained, also *unknown.* Consequently, not consoling, redeeming, or obligating: how could something unknown obligate us? (Gray morning. The first yawn of reason. The cockcrow of positivism).
> 5. The "true" world—an idea which is no longer good for anything, not even obligating—an idea which has become

> useless and superfluous—*consequently*, a refuted idea: let us abolish it! (Bright day; breakfast; return of *bon sens* and cheerfulness; Plato's embarrassed blush; pandemonium of all free spirits).
> 6. The true world—we have abolished. What world has remained? The apparent one perhaps. But no! *With the true world we have also abolished the apparent one.* (Noon; moment of the briefest shadow; end of the longest error; high point of humanity; INCIPIT ZARATHUSTRA).[39]

This is the history of a number of successive and related philosophical theories. They begin with (1) the Platonic idea of a real world access which is restricted to the philosopher. The belief in this other world is motivated by a skepticism about the common sense view of the world we experience. This theory is gradually replaced by or rather incorporated into Christianity (2) but with an unhappy transformation. The true world is not even possible in or through this world. We must see these views, as Nietzsche suggests, according to the psychology which produced them. The Platonic view comes from a noble perspective, it is the seizing of power through an idea. Plato becomes the privileged bearer of or seeker after truth. In Christianity the desire becomes more disguised. With Kant (3) we lose this promised world. It becomes empty, unknown, and yet it is supposed to retain a moral effect.

When positivism (4) comes on the scene, we simply take Kant at his word and give up the real, noumenal world, but not the quest. Without God, we still try to construct a world where we have the certainty and truth found in the previous perspectives, or at least part of them. Finally (5), we give up the "true" world altogether, including its insidious traces in positive science. The end of the Platonic error, the beginning of a new view of life. The true world and the apparent one which is logically dependent upon it vanish. And instead, we can reconstruct or recreate a world here which does not rely upon either the idea of another world (because we are so pessimistic about the one we inhabit), or that forces us to look on this world as apparent, therefore always in relation to another, and therefore always denigrated or existing with dependence on the other idea. Instead, we abolish both.

What is the world we are left with? The world we are left with is the world of our life; as we experience it in living, in our activities. We find again and again in Nietzsche's writings the idea that what is attractive about some individual, for example, Johann Wolfgang Goethe, or some people, for example, the Greeks, is that they knew how to make knowledge or thought serve life. We have to explore what this means. *The Uses and Disadvantages of History for Life* begins with a quotation from Goethe: "In any case, I hate everything that merely instructs me without augmenting or directly invigorating my activity."[40] Nietzsche endorses this sentiment at the beginning of his essay.[41] We find repeated reference to the value of a philosophy which does not merely instruct but makes us more alive. But what is this life? I think it is fairly clear what it is not. It is not the world of the metaphysician, nor even the epistemologist. It is nothing conceived; instead, it is lived. But although we have rejected the possibility of the transcendental world Nietzsche is equally unwilling to give us, in substitution, a view of a stable, material one: the world of the empiricists or positivists.

In dealing with what Nietzsche means by life, it makes some sense to try to read him as a phenomenologist. Certainly he was not a phenomenologist like Husserl, who was still looking for objectivity and was still stuck with the positivists, who had not learned to give up the features of truth and philosophy which both came into being under an absurd notion of "the world." Nietzsche was a phenomenologist in the sense that in phenomena, in experience as we live it, lies a truth or unity between knower and known which is not reducible or, rather, divisible into either subject or object. This is not to say that the unity of life and experience is an unproblematic notion, nor, as I hope I have suggested, that life is some primitive given, pure of theoretical constructions and corruptions. Nietzsche says:

> Words are but symbols for the relations of things to one another and to us; nowhere do they touch upon absolute truth .... Through words and concepts we shall never reach beyond the wall of relations, to some sort of fabulous primal ground of things.[42]

Nietzsche is neither a romantic nor a naturalist or realist.

We know from what we have seen so far that certain philosophical views which privilege reason and denigrate experience are, in Nietzsche's terms, bad or "unhealthy." We will return to examine the meaning of this characterization. He wants to posit a counter-image of life which gives back to experience its fullness and richness. Christian morality, with its other-worldly perspective, turned us away from life and especially from the sensual elements which were a part of it.

> Christian morality ... that which *corrupted* humanity .... That one taught men to despise the very first instincts of life; that one mendaciously invented a "soul," a "spirit" to ruin the body; that one taught men to experience the presupposition of life, sexuality, as something unclean; that one looks for the evil principle in what is most profoundly necessary for growth, in *severe* self-love (this very word constitutes slander); that, conversely, one regards the typical signs of decline and contradiction of the instincts, the "selfless," the loss of a center of gravity, "depersonalization" and "neighbor love" (*addiction* to the neighbor) as the *higher* value—what am I saying?—the *absolute* value![43]

The positive image of life is expressed in an aesthetic or sensual context because it is primarily in this context that it has been denied. But is there some real life?

Yes and no. Nietzsche can only appeal to experience by pointing to something which we feel or live. He tells us what it is not. This has helped him to evaluate those theories we have examined which distort some of the realities of our condition. But "our condition" is not the human condition, nor is it the condition of, for example, Sartre or Heidegger. Nothing in it is static or fixed, nor is it dependent upon a metaphysics of a person. We are in a situation, in fact many situations, over which we cannot generalize because of the concreteness in our individual, although culturally informed, life. The condition I am trying to pay special attention to here is the position of a reformer within a culture. How do we have an idea of change without the idea of free will, with the idea that we are in a culture, etc.? Our condition, then, is that of Nietzsche and some other "free spirits" or "higher men" who are interested in change and in looking at culture from a new or projected "outside"

The above passage from the *Twilight of the Idols* not only makes us reconsider this view of the world and hence of life, but also reveals a technique or strategy which Nietzsche employs repeatedly. We have seen this strategy already in connection with "necessity and accident," and we now see it with "true and apparent" worlds. I am referring to his undermining of established dichotomies.[44] The point is not the inversion of the hierarchy; it is "a transformation of the hierarchical structure itself," as Derrida says describing Heidegger's interpretation of this passage. Nietzsche effectively destroys not only the idea of the true world, but perhaps more importantly, the idea of an apparent one. Why? The view of the world of our sense experience and lived experience as "apparent" rested on at least the possibility of there being a real, absolute one. It was in relation to the true world that the world of our life became merely "apparent" and unworthy of trust. By accepting that there is no true world we undermine the designation of the world of sense experience as an apparent or illusory world, and we are left not with the apparent one which was defined and denigrated by the "otherworldly" but with the only world there has been all along, although always under different descriptions, the world of our knowing, feeling, and living. This is the world of which we are a part and with which we are connected.

The attempt to find a true world reveals a pessimism about life:

> To invent fables about a world "other" than this one has no meaning at all, unless an instinct of slander, detraction, and suspicion against life has gained the upper hand in us: in that case, we avenge ourselves against life with a phantasmagoria of "another," a "better" life.[45]

This is, according to Nietzsche, a symptom of the decline of our culture, and its pessimism needs to be countered with an affirmative, Dionysian, vision. That other-worldliness was:

> ... the degenerating instinct that turns against life with subterranean vengefulness ... versus a formula for the highest

> affirmation, born of fullness, of overfullness, a Yes-saying without reservation, even to suffering, even to guilt, even to everything that is questionable and strange in existence.
>
> This ultimate, most joyous, most wantonly extravagant Yes to life represents not only the highest insight, but also the *deepest*, that which is most strictly confirmed and born out by truth and science ....[46]

Another point we have considered has to do with the critique of Christianity, and specifically of the Christian God. Creating a conception of the world which replaces the world in which we live is a common characteristic of many cultures. But, according to Nietzsche, it has many unhappy consequences. The world in which we live has some features which make it seem less desirable than some of the visions that are competing with it. In it, change is constant, animals live and die. Human beings, as both animals and conscious beings, see death as not just a feature of reality but as something we would like to avoid or at least avoid worrying about. Strong cultural forces have attempted to deny the obvious "realities" associated with change in our world. We find a life-denying tendency in the ancient world and Christianity, but also in other cultures. Nietzsche mentions that both Buddhist and Indian world views involve life-denying other-worldliness.

The world of Christianity is a spiritual world or at least gives a priority to a world of that kind. In that world there is completion and intelligibility. This world, the world of life which Nietzsche refers to, is in the process of becoming. It is in flux. The latter world is one which we experience and whose features are intuitively plausible to us even if not always pleasant.

The Platonic and Christian divorce between these worlds encourages belief in certain notions of truth and reality. A complete view is found in each world, a view which comes from outside of time. The world exists as a reality independent of our experience of it. This is how we came to understand the "demand for certainty" which Nietzsche criticizes so vehemently in the passages discussed above. The view that certainty in knowing was attainable, was tied to a certain picture of the world. The critical characteristic of that picture was that there were some features of it which were static and that, therefore, we could have certain, timeless knowledge about them.

Nietzsche doubts whether we can have knowledge about a truth or reality which is so construed. He doubts whether such knowledge is attainable (or desirable). Reason and order are left to the "true" world, but we have found that philosophers and scientists still look for the characteristics which were associated with discredited beliefs long after it is recognized that "God is dead." Kant is someone who still attempts to reconcile both worlds; the world of experience and the world he believes lies behind it.

The death of God suggests the end of all non-perspectival knowing. There are still many views of perspectival or limited knowing which can be considered. We have seen how many of them were discredited by Nietzsche because they retained some vestige of an illegitimate perspective: the trans-experiential. We have, also, begun to consider some of the consequences to morality. We need to look further into these and to consider the historical, cultural, and psychological motivations that lie behind the desire for this other world of reason and control.

Nietzsche used the metaphor of the death of God to do a lot of destructive work, and one of the things he did was give us an image of the consequences of the collapse of an objective, disinterested, or other-worldly perspective. Nietzsche, as we have seen, tied the two together. We looked at the passage called "The Madman" which showed some of the consequences for Western morality, of taking the belief in the death of that God seriously. The frustration the Madman expresses is the result of our unwillingness to consider the consequences of the loss of what once stood behind our moral values. To the madman, these consequences suggested a task which was frightening in its extent: a reevaluation of all values. We have to become gods, that is, we have to become the givers or creators of value. The Madman finds this intimidating. (In other passages, Nietzsche finds it exhilarating and liberating).[47]

In Nietzsche's work we have seen an emphasis on or trust in experience. This emphasis is necessary because of previous philosophical systems' distrust of the world of appearance and becoming in their quest for absolute knowledge. In contrast, Nietzsche is saying that we must focus on life as we live it. Nothing exists behind the appearances. In a way, like many other philosophers, he is just taking the Kantian limitation seriously. But we focus on "this" world not grudgingly, as some lesser alternative, but with the realization that this is and has been the only alternative, all along. The world of becoming did not become the world after Kant did away with the world of being, it always was the world. Given this, speculations about another world have quite a different character, and their effects are metaphorical instead of metaphysical. When we find that philosophy must deal with the world of our experience, and always must have done so, an interesting question arises. How are we to look at earlier metaphysics that claimed to deal with this other world? A new story is needed in order to construct an interpretation of what was going on, and in order to find out what of use can be found in the previous methods of doing philosophy. This is what Nietzsche was doing in the passages from the *Twilight of the Idols* and *Philosophy in the Tragic Age of the Greeks*.

One of the less felicitous consequences of looking at Nietzsche's philosophy in this way (by beginning with the radical and even vitriolic attacks upon Christianity and then expanding them into their place in his more general criticism of philosophy) is that we tend to think of his task as simply one of substituting a new correct way of thinking for these earlier erroneous ways, the correct way, naturally, being his way. In a sense this is true, but in a far more important sense it is false. It is true to the extent that Nietzsche obviously believes what he is saying. He thinks that we cannot go back to metaphysics, transcendentalism or even positivism, so he believes that his critique is "true." He also believes that the new values and value schemes which he proposes are better, at least better when they are posited against their historical and cultural framework.

The "problem" is that beliefs and truths are contextualized. There is no privileged position, as we have said before, and Nietzsche's own values are not immune to this "problem," if we choose to see it as a problem. Nietzsche does not see it as a problem; he sees it as a given. We must necessarily see things from a perspective and this is, in fact, what allows for knowing. It is not merely an unfortunate limitation on our knowledge.[48] What, then, makes Nietzsche's view more compelling? It is obviously more compelling to him because it escapes many of the "errors" and "unhealthy" psychological motivations which are present in the theories he is criticizing.

Nietzsche does not believe that there is one true way of seeing the world—not even his way. The business of the philosopher and artist is to create new ways of interpreting our life and singling out aspects of existence for examination or affirmation. None of these will, however, be the definitive answer because that is not what the nature of the enterprise is or can be—precisely because we cannot now ignore life in its changing modes, and because we have given up the search for the true world which was ahistorical, asocial, certain, and necessary. In other words, we stopped trying to put the life we lived into a formula which denied most of our experience but gave us the illusion of security and control. And we have given up the attempt to reduce experience to one aspect of it.

But, once again, we need to realize that we did not give up Christianity merely because it was false, if we take "false" in some conventional sense. We gave it up because of the dire consequences it had for life and living. Christianity, and all metaphysics for that matter, resulted in a pessimistic view of life, particularly of sensual life. Nietzsche gives an example of this in *Ecce Homo*. Here, "vice" is Christian virtue. This switch in meaning is part of an inversion of values which Nietzsche is trying to bring about.

> I use the word "vice" in my fight against every kind of antinature or, if you prefer pretty words, idealism. The proposition reads: "The preaching of chastity amounts to a public incitement to antinature. Every kind of contempt for sex, every impurification of it by means of the concept 'impure,' is the crime *par excellence* against life—is the real sin against the holy spirit of life."[49]

These Christian "vices" directed our energies and our concerns away from this world to where our energies were wasted on other-worldly speculation. Nietzsche calls this turning away from life "decadence." Typically he is reversing the usual sense of the term. "Decadence," under Christianity, meant a degeneration into sensuality and emotion. For Nietzsche it means a move away from life, especially, away from sense and emotion to reason or some other abstraction.

As we have seen, most philosophy and science has until now tried to know by controlling, manipulating, and appropriating. In the notes collected as *The Will to Power* Nietzsche writes: "The entire apparatus of knowledge is an apparatus for abstraction and simplification directed not at knowledge but at taking possession of things."[50] This is not Nietzsche's idea of what philosophy should be. To him, such a desire betrays the psychology of the person who has it—it betrays a discomfort with the world as it is, that is *not* orderly, law-governed, or God-governed (providence). But what is life as it is? As we have seen, there is no life-as-it-is in any primordial sense or any neutral sense or even in any *one* involved sense. Life involves a certain uncertainty and lack of control, but what is perhaps more vital to our understanding is that we always are acting within a "false" description of the world. In other words, we construct a fiction about what life is like that explains, justifies, denigrates or praises certain elements of life. We, as philosophers and priests and people, produce a culture and that culture has a view of life. We are always in a situation, even in the midst of our revisions and critiques.

It is obvious to Nietzsche that we construct our world. That is our act of creation: Not the act of making the world, but re-making it in our conceptions and interpretations. All the stories of the true world which we considered earlier are part of the creative product of Western civilization. To realize this is to change the way we think about the nature of the historical, evaluative, and philosophical project. We are neither involved in discovering preexistent values the way the Platonist or Christian would describe them, nor of simply inventing them according to fixed scientific standards of human psychology.

This should help to clear up some of the confusion people feel when they encounter passages where Nietzsche praises Christ or Judaism. Since many critics see Nietzsche's destructive program without really understanding his deeper methodological critique, they take him to be simply favoring early Greek over Christian culture. They then find in his comments praising Western religion a deep puzzle or paradox. Western religion is praised as a cultural product, as our contribution, as a manifestation of our will to power. In addition to art; philosophies, religions, and political systems are the creative products of a culture. For example, Nietzsche praises the Old Testament as the great aesthetic projection of our cultural values. As such, it embodies what we as a people have affirmed. The fact that much of this is no longer useful to us, as a people moving into a future and living in a different world, does not minimize the achievement of this cultural creation.

In a like manner, all aspects of Greek culture are not praiseworthy, but they are what is left to us and allow us to understand a quite different world. They provide an alternative model to some aspects of the Christian culture which have ceased to be fruitful, and we may consider them as actual alternatives because they once existed even if for another people. But Nietzsche is obviously not so naive as to think that we can go back to that culture, nor is he so romantic about it to find that a desirable alternative. He is quite aware of the brutality and pessimism of the early Greek culture, and also aware of the price that the Greek people paid for what they produced.

Nietzsche is an unconventional thinker in that he both acknowledges cultural historical changes, which makes him unpopular with the transcendentalists; and resists putting these changes into a formula, which displeases the Hegelians and Marxists. For Nietzsche, what may be required for an age and place will not necessarily be helpful to another. There is no pattern to historical movement. There is nothing to comfort us, nothing certain, nothing to make us more secure. This openness with respect to history is not something which is likely to make him popular with other philosophers. He rejects what they most often take as their chief attributes and distinguishing characteristics: the special place of the logical faculty (what Nietzsche occasionally calls the hypertrophy of reason), the "fact" that their truths are ahistorical or asocial, and the justification of the empirical method are some examples of this.

We have been examining, so far, what the task of the philosopher is in a time when metaphysics has become first suspect and then impossible, and this at a time when the tasks of philosophy have turned epistemological, have turned in upon themselves to examine the knower and the knower's relation to the known. At a time when the methods of positive science (as we have seen represented in the philosopher of desperate knowledge) are fast becoming the norm of the European sciences or disciplines, Nietzsche is already criticizing them as atavistic! What, then, is the business of the philosopher, when we have given up both "reality" and "truth"?

> History and the natural sciences were necessary to combat the middle ages: knowledge vs. faith. We now oppose knowledge with *art*: return to life! Mastery of the knowledge drive! Strengthening of the moral and aesthetic instincts![51]

Truth, knowledge, and certainty give way to value giving, value making. Even, and in some ways, especially, scientific knowledge is evaluated psychologically in terms of physiology or pathology, and this is all a consequence of giving up the possibility of a transcendental perspective and a letting go of the other world—an abandonment of the attempt to control—to make the world conform to our expectation of it—to our desires and needs whether conceptual or material.

This life or world of our experience is not something we can define or encapsulate. One of Nietzsche's main criticisms of logic or reason-mongering is that any attempt to fit experience into a formula distorts it. In *The Will to Power* he says:

> Logic is bound to the condition: assume there are identical cases. In fact, to make possible logical thinking and inferences, this condition must first be treated fictitiously as fulfilled. That is: the will to logical truth can be carried through only after a fundamental *falsification* of all events is assumed ....[52]

Part of this problem comes from having used as a model an idea of knowledge which, as we saw in the case of Parmenides, is borrowed from mathematics. Even in this context it relied on fictions.

> *The number.* The laws of numbers were invented on the basis of the initially prevailing error that there are various identical things (but actually there is nothing identical) or at least that

> there are things (but there is no "thing"). The assumption of multiplicity always presumes that there is *something*, which occurs repeatedly. But this is just where error rules; even here, we invent entities, unities that do not exist .... To a world that is *not* our idea, the laws of numbers are completely inapplicable: they are valid only in the human world.[53]

They are valid in a world which is our idea, but not in the world which is part of our experience.

The life of which Nietzsche repeatedly speaks cannot be captured by definition. In order to communicate this idea it will have to be shown in some other way. This is what makes it so difficult to explain. Heidegger has at least an analogous difficulty in communicating when he talks about the primordial, although his idea is not the same as life experience. The primordial is not something which can be communicated by propositional logic or argument. One cannot argue for its existence; indeed, it would be absurd to try, for that would be missing the point. If someone is to be convinced it will not be by a deductive argument, but by an appeal to experience. There is no alternative.

Life is that thing which is going on "in" you, which you are afraid might end, which is the focus of the many layers of your experience. It includes our consciousness, but also our feelings and sensations which are not located mentally (that is, not the consciousness Descartes would describe, nor Plato if he had such a notion). Nietzsche is talking about the embodied, feeling being as a whole experienced from within: not a being in which there is a radical divorce between intellect and feeling or desire. In order to have someone else understand this idea, we must make an analogy between what we are experiencing and describing as our life, and what we are confident is the experience of others. This appeal is not to our mental life, but rather to our entire experienced life, which means: the sensations we are having, the fear we feel, the argument we are trying to follow. Nor are these discrete in our experience, although it is true that they are separable in an act of conceptualization.

Let us now return to the quotation which began this chapter and see what it means in the light of what we have hitherto explored.

> "Saying Yes to life even in its strangest and hardest problems ...." In this sense I have the right to understand myself as the first *tragic philosopher*—that is, the most extreme opposite and antipode of a pessimistic philosopher. Before me this transposition of the Dionysian into a philosophical pathos did not exist ....[54]

Why does Nietzsche call himself a tragic philosopher? For Nietzsche, tragedy in its highest forms had two characteristics that are relevant in the present analysis. All aspects of life are considered: the pleasant and the unpleasant, and those aspects in our control and those outside of it. Tragedy is not pessimistic because it does not need to suppress the truth but rather only embellish it. Nietzsche has been critical of an opposing trend, a true pessimism which found it necessary to disparage the aspects of life which were outside of our control: it did this at the expense of creating a new world theologically, metaphysically, or rationally (positivism).

> *The philosopher of tragic knowledge.* He masters the uncontrolled knowledge drive, though not by means of a new metaphysics. He establishes no new faith. He considers it *tragic* that the ground of metaphysics has been withdrawn, and he will never permit himself to be satisfied with the motley whirling game of the sciences.[55]

Again, his criticism is not that the world is fictional or untrue, but instead that this is an overly pessimistic view. "One must even *will illusion*—that is what is tragic." This pessimism disconnects us from the ways in which we can be attached to life. Nietzsche wants us to celebrate life. "He cultivates a new life; he returns to art its rights."

Chapter Two

MORALITY AND THE SWITCH FROM THE PERSPECTIVE OF A JUDGE TO THAT OF A PARTICIPANT

> *Private morality, world morality.* Since man no longer believes that a God is guiding the destinies of the world as a whole, or that, despite all apparent twists, the path of mankind is leading somewhere glorious, men must set themselves ecumenical goals, embracing the whole earth. The older morality, namely Kant's, demands from the individual those actions that one desires from all men—a nice, a naive idea, as if everyone without further ado would know which manner of action would benefit the whole of mankind, that is, which actions were desirable at all .... In any event, if mankind is to keep from destroying itself ..., we must discover first a *knowledge of the conditions of culture*, a knowledge surpassing all previous knowledge, as a scientific [*wissenschaftlicher*] standard for ecumenical goals. This is the enormous task of the great minds [*Geister*] of the next century.[1]

In the first chapter of this work we looked at the way Nietzsche uses the "death of God" as a metaphor. The purpose of examining this "event" was to look at Nietzsche's views about its consequences for epistemology and metaphysics. It became evident that Nietzsche's criticism of the Christian God was not just aimed at a theological principle. Nietzsche was interested in showing the way in which the idea of that God has affected the goals of philosophy, religion, and morality.

We now know that Nietzsche wanted to show us that human knowledge is not like the Christian God's. That God was considered to be all-knowing. It lacked both the limiting and the enabling powers which are a part of having a perspective, of being in a situation. Our knowledge is necessarily perspectival, limited, and interested. We have seen that Nietzsche believed the "loss" of the transcendental viewpoint, (represented symbolically by this God), was a "tragedy." By this, Nietzsche meant that if such a view (or being) were possible, its loss would have been tragic indeed.

Perspectiveless knowledge usually means knowledge from the outside, that which is not distorted by the knower being in a situation, although it may mean knowledge of all perspectives simultaneously. Nietzsche can understand our having the desire to have such knowledge, but, unfortunately, we do not have it. Knowledge of this type is impossible because of the nature of the knower. We found that Nietzsche believed both "God" and the "true" world were a "lie." In learning this truth we both lost something and we did not. We didn't lose what we seem to have lost, namely, the God and the transcendental perspective. We have not really lost that; all we had was the lie in the first place. Although we did not lose this, it was a comforting lie. As a consequence we lost the effects of having this shared belief, this illusion. One of the qualities of our creative illusions is their psychological effects, so, in that sense, we lost a great deal.

Perspectival or relational knowledge is not an utterly new notion in the history of philosophy. Nietzsche talks of the importance of knowing things in relation to the knower which characterized many early Greek thinkers. But, since Parmenides and certainly Plato, philosophers have tried to achieve a "god's eye view" of the world. The result has been an other-worldliness—a preoccupation with notions and ideals which are not capable of fitting in with the world we experience in our everyday life. This results in schemes and world views which are both false and pernicious.

Nietzsche has concluded that all knowing is perspectival. He discredited the god who represented non-perspectival knowing. He did this first by noticing "that the belief in the Christian God has become unbelievable."[2] He further undermined the belief by unmasking some of the motivations of those who created it. Christian metaphysics and epistemology (and those of other philosophers which resembled them) were then looked at in a psychological and ultimately historical context. The result was that we saw disguised remnants of ancient and Christian metaphysics and epistemology. Nietzsche thinks we have to abandon all of this in order to completely root out what he calls "Christianity," but what we have now discovered goes far beyond this, to include a great deal of philosophy including various forms of empiricism which could hardly be called "Christian."

If we cannot do metaphysics, and critical philosophy and positivism are equally suspect, what do philosophers do? What Nietzsche does, to give an example, is begin to legitimate a perspective that is inside of history.

> *Happiness of the historian.*—"When we hear ingenious metaphysicians and back worldsmen talk, we others may feel that we are the 'poor in spirit,' but we also feel that ours is the kingdom of Heaven of change, with spring and autumn, winter and summer, and that theirs is the backworld—with its gray, frosty, unending mist and shadow."—Thus a man spoke to himself while walking in the morning sun: one in whom history again and again transforms not only his spirit but also his heart, and who, in contrast to the metaphysicians, is happy to harbor in himself, not "an immortal soul," but *many mortal souls*.[3]

The historian in the parable is not interested in timeless truths, but rather with the individual lives of people which take place in time. He looks at his task at first as something less grand than that of the metaphysician, but then, as one which opens many possibilities to him. This dual aspect of the philosopher's new task: the loss of the "grand" calling and the tremendous liberation of being recalled to a world of life, is represented again and again in Nietzsche's work.

Nietzsche gives us a combination of historical and psychological accounts of the origins of beliefs, practices, and values. The psychological explanations help to establish the plausibility of the historical accounts. Thus, in the example of discovering the motivation behind the creation of another world, he considers the possibility of rancor being part of the Christian's desire for a world of judgment. This motivation may seem more plausible to us when we think both about how the double threat of heaven and hell works, and the unhappy situation in which the early Christians found themselves. In addition, Nietzsche gives historical information which establishes that vengeance is part of the reward for Christian patience and docility.

Nietzsche's use of a historical or what he calls a "genealogical" philosophical method makes a difference. He is introducing into philosophy two methods of analysis or understanding which have, for the most part, stood outside of it. History was supposed to be done by historians, and psychology by psychologists. But, Nietzsche is introducing these types of explanations into philosophy. He did this above in the account of the history of ancient Greek philosophy. He will do it also in the case of morality in *The Genealogy of Morals.* First let us look at what a genealogy is.

A genealogy aims at uncovering a genesis or starting point for a practice or conception which we already have. It is a historical understanding, an interpretation of history, but, unlike historical methods which claim or attempt to be objective accounts of events, the aim of genealogy is a liberation. The genealogy aims at a liberation from some established way of seeing a practice or institution, or from some habit of conceptualizing. It is an aid to reevaluation. The point of doing this critical analysis is practical in the sense that it attempts to change the way we think and live.

In *The Gay Science*, Nietzsche bequeaths a task to the "Industrious." This task is a critical historical analysis of certain human relations and institutions. For example, he states that we lack a history of avarice, of envy, of the dialectic of marriage and friendship. There remains an enormous amount of work to be done by philosophers and historians: "so far, all that has given color to existence still lacks a history."[4] Even in areas where philosophers have traditionally acknowledged a problem or task, for example, in the examination of the "conditions of existence," he claims the work has not been exhaustive. So this overwhelming job is only for the industrious.

In later works, Nietzsche attempts to remedy some of these deficiencies. *The Genealogy of Morals* has an analysis of punishment, of guilt, and of asceticism. He uses his philological skills to help him uncover the origin of the modern Western conception of morality. Nietzsche finds part of an answer to the question of how our morality arose in the way in which moral concepts have changed their meaning over time. The topics Nietzsche decides to work on are topics in which he has an interest, and about which he has suspicions. The topic of a genealogy should be one which arises from the particular interests of the inquirer. The emphasis in this method is placed on the attachment of the thinker and the topic. The motivation for the inquiry is then explained in terms of a desire to reevaluate or re-think the topic. The genealogy consists in tracing a practice back to its inception. Because of the way the question is asked, there will be limitations on the answer. The inquiry is neither free from presuppositions nor value free. No inquiry is.

Nietzsche assumes a connection between knowing, evaluating, and doing. He does this quite simply, by refusing to give a reductionist account of life and experience. Hence the categories which philosophers use and which correspond to these separated "modes" of existence or types of human action, such as epistemology, value theory, action theory, must necessarily be seen as artificial constructions and divisions which we are imposing on the life we live. Part of Nietzsche's program is a critical analysis of the various sources of these divisions. His motivations will become evident as we consider his criticism of objectivisms in more detail.

The purpose of this genealogy is to liberate us from some established practice. This kind of knowledge, the story we tell of the genesis of a practice, is instrumental for our escaping from or reforming that practice. The motivation for the inquiry that results in the genealogy is a kind of suspicion. This suspicion may come from our reflection upon some cultural phenomenon. The nineteenth century's turn away from God, especially as a source of explanation and justification, is an example of one cultural change which Nietzsche observes and uses. The "death of God" provides the impetus for reading back into history a new story of the genesis of our moral concepts. Now we know that the origins of the moral concepts cannot be traced to the will of the creator. But they did originate somewhere. Knowing where they come from might be helpful in our re-evaluation of their worth to us now. From our vantage point in history, some practice comes to be regarded with suspicion in the light of current or contemporary understanding. In our attempt to liberate ourselves from such a practice we construct an alternative story to the established or official one. The aim is not merely destructive. The destruction, in this case (perhaps in all of the cases), is accomplished, previously, simply by the lack of belief. The meaningful element is Nietzsche's realization of the consequences of the lack of faith, namely the loss of a justification for many of the moral values on Western society. So, instead of mere destruction, the account aims at a reconstruction, at least partially, by means of history. Implicit in the critical re-reading or re-writing of history is an attempt to recover what can be of use. In this case, what values are worthwhile will be decided by appealing to new criteria (Nietzsche is fond of using "healthy" or "life-affirming)."[5] These criteria are the tentative values of the inquirer.

This brings us to another issue, the place of the inquirer in this work. The theorist is not separated from the one who must act, in fact, the motivation for the theoretical understanding arises in a historical context and from serious issues involving the life of the inquirer. Having philosophical problems begins by having "practical" problems. The problems are crucial, they must be answered, and we answer them in living. The person who does the genealogy has a purpose. The fact that the observer is interested, and has a purpose, does not make the task less weighty or less true, it makes it vital. I will return to this matter.

Up to this point we have simply surveyed some important aspects of Nietzsche's methodology. In these genealogies we must acknowledge that the inquirer is in history, that the vital issues come from questions arising in living. Life or experience is the irreducible starting point and the appeal to experience must be our means of adjudicating.

In Nietzsche's work we find the roots of a genealogical critique of philosophy itself, as well as of Christian morality. In the previous chapter we looked at two examples of this in the history of philosophy. Because of the history of the discipline, Nietzsche expects that philosophers will be resistant to his methods. He says, "Philosophers are prejudiced against appearance, change, pain, death, the corporeal, the senses, fate and bondage, the aimless."[6] "They believe first in Absolute knowledge, in knowledge for the sake of knowledge, in an association between virtue and happiness, in the comprehensibility of human actions."[7] "What do philosophers lack? An historical sense, knowledge of physiology."[8] Nietzsche's philosophy is supposed to stand against these prejudices of philosophers. The work of philosophers must be read as an interested story. The philosopher's interests and motivations, however well dressed in the guise of disinterest or objectivity, make it necessary for us to look back at them with fresh eyes. This is part of the demythologizing which takes place when doing a genealogy.

Again, the genealogy is not merely a destructive endeavor, it is a retelling with a purpose: to transform history and to consider the contemporary understanding and valuing of a practice. So that when we do a genealogical critique of philosophy, it is not to undermine the enterprise, but to find in the tradition what is helpful for us. So we retell the story, a different story, in order to further our purposes and legitimate our enterprises. The genealogies are not the final answer to what doing philosophy is or should be. They are preparatory. But they are also not neutral; they suggest what the interests and concerns of philosophy should be. Remember that Nietzsche believes all philosophies have always had these features, but they were not previously acknowledged.

In the previous chapter, I spoke of the fact that Nietzsche was using an extended sense of "morality" and "ethics." He did not want to limit the morally relevant by demanding a degree of abstraction or by restricting issues to those of a conventional notion of importance. In this chapter I would like to look at Nietzsche's critique of contemporary morality. We will first put that morality into its historical context by means of a genealogy, and then use the information from that analysis to look at Nietzsche's reevaluation of contemporary morality and his positive recommendations. These will then be tied in with the other positive re-valuings which for the most part concern themselves with early Greek culture and specifically those which are a part of Nietzsche's other genealogy: the genealogy of contemporary aesthetic value which we will look at in the analysis of *The Birth of Tragedy*.

What I would like to concern myself with is Nietzsche's analysis of a possible origin of contemporary European morality. This will concentrate on the way it is represented in *The Genealogy of Morals* and *Beyond Good and Evil*, §§260-261, because in these cases his remarks are purposely made in a historical context. But other texts will be referred to, as well. The task of placing morality in a historical narrative is relevant to the eventual re-valuation of values he wishes to bring about. He discovers this origin in a system of values which arose in a particular historical context. By looking at the etymology of certain moral concepts, "good," "bad," and "evil," he finds a way to trace the manner in which values changed over time. In the case of the word "good," he finds an affinity between the earliest notion of "good" and that of "nobility." "Good" is used to designate both a group of people and a quality. This suggests to him that there was an ancient connection between the concept of the good and the class of people who employed it: the nobility. It seems that good was first associated with a person or type of person instead of an act. Nietzsche says, "It is obvious that moral designations were everywhere first applied to *human beings* and only later, derivatively, to actions."[9] This is seen to be in contrast to the contemporary understanding of moral evaluation (in for example, Kant or modern liberal theory) in which ideas or concepts are associated more often with an action than with a person or class of people. In fact, the action itself is seen as having the primary relevance in evaluation and often precisely the action irrespective of the person who performed it. This is part of the modern notion of justice or fairness. Moral evaluations apply universally and an action is right or wrong regardless of who performs it.

In contemporary Western culture, we often associate morality with a set of prescriptions which guide our actions. Quite often these are negative, they require that we do not do something: Do not steal, do not murder, do not harm anyone. Less often they ask that we do something: Honor our parents, participate in our government, help people in need. This way of speaking about morality suggests that certain actions are wrong and certain actions are right—in and of themselves. If this were so, then we, as moral individuals, would have to find out what the good actions were and do them. Morality could be largely a matter of acting in conformity with the good or, in Kant's understanding, in obedience to a moral law. The good could be binding on us in a number of ways: for example, in virtue of its source in political, or religious beliefs. We would do "the right thing" only if for some reason we wanted to be "moral." This conception of morality is fairly specific and restricted. Nietzsche gives his own summary of such a view "when a human being judges '*this is right*' and then infers '*therefore it must be done*,' and then proceeds to *do* what he has thus recognized as right and designated as necessary—then the essence of his action is *moral*."[10] This is not a view Nietzsche endorses; it is one he caricatures. As we shall see, he wants to look at a variety of moralities, and expands the notion of the moral well beyond this rather restrictive one.

Nietzsche caricatures many of the positions which he attacks. He is unfair in his assessment of many authors. In spite of this, we need to look at those aspects of them he is criticizing. The purpose in doing so is not to get a good or fair reading of Kant or whoever, but to see what Nietzsche is trying to say. Since he often says it in the course of combat with a historical figure, it is necessary to consider even his more cavalier remarks. This examination includes remarks which some people find gratuitously offensive, yet whose point is significant either rhetorically or substantially.

Within this type of morality, a transcendental justification is often offered for the fact that certain actions are right and others wrong. By "transcendental" Nietzsche means a justification which goes beyond this world, the world of our experience or life. This justification can be found in another world (the realm of perfect form), another being (a god), or by the use of a faculty which claims to be able to transcend the biases and irregularities of the world of experience (by reason). On this view, a morality is not seen as having a history. It transcends history. And this transcendence is part of what is seen as its greatest asset: good will always be good and bad will remain bad. This will be true wherever one is, whenever one lived, and regardless of any other circumstance. From what we have seen of Nietzsche's critiques so far, it should be obvious that he will be critical of this type of thinking. One reason he finds it unpalatable is, it demands that values should be radically divorced from their context.

Let us consider Nietzsche's comments on Kant's idea of a categorical imperative. This is a paradigmatic case of a moral system which will produce precepts without a reliance on the context. In fact, one thing the categorical imperative does is to remove each action from its context. It does this by means of the formulation of a maxim, and by means of the universalizing process. The maxim is to be formalized in a way sufficiently general that it applies to more than the individual case which gave birth to it. Thus, even before the universalizing process, there is a generalizing process. Kant is not terribly specific about how this is to be done. The test of the categorical imperative is then applied. The method for determining the right action is particularly aimed at the elimination of context (by taking the problem into a detached logical space). This does not guarantee that one will do the right action, but it does (according to Kant) insure that one knows what it is!

Nietzsche wants to criticize this notion of morality. To do this he makes another equally controversial move; he puts this moral theory, that is, Kant's, into the context of its creation. This time it is not only in the historical, cultural context, but actually looking at it in connection with its author: a psychological context. This move is controversial precisely because by doing it he connects the creator and the creation. This violates a philosophical convention. In *Beyond Good and Evil*, §187, Nietzsche says: "Even apart from the value of such claims as 'there is a categorical imperative in us,' one can still always ask: what does such a claim tell us about the man who makes it?"[11] He wants to evaluate the work by evaluating what such a morality does for the person who created it. This puts it in a kind of pragmatic framework. It is not only Kant's, but, as we shall see, all moralities which should be considered in this way.

Hence Nietzsche violates many contemporary philosophical conventions: what we have come to call the genetic fallacy is one of the more obvious. This states that the genesis of the action is not relevant to its evaluation.[12] He asks what a theory tells us about its author. In fact, he gives us a catalogue of what a variety of moral theories in the past have done for their creators.

> There are moralities which are meant to justify their creator before others. Other moralities are meant to calm him and lead him to be satisfied with himself. With yet others he wants to crucify himself and humiliate himself. With others he wants to wreak revenge, with others conceal himself, with others transfigure himself and place himself way up, at a distance. This morality is used by its creator to forget, that one to have others forget him or something about him. Some moralists want to vent their power and creative whims on humanity; ...[13]

If we do not have a terribly difficult time thinking of examples of the types of moralities which he is talking about, then we have reason to believe there is at least some truth in what he says. But to return to the issue at hand, Nietzsche goes on to say: "some others, perhaps including Kant, suggest with their morality: 'What deserves respect in me is that I can obey—and you *ought* not to be different from me.'" This gives away Kant's slave-like desire for the universal, "if I must do this you must too!" This is, as we shall see, a quality of the slavish Christian morality.

Again, in regard to the categorical imperative Nietzsche writes:

> What? You admire the categorical imperative within you? This "firmness" of your so-called moral judgment? This "unconditional" feeling that "here everyone must judge as I do?" Rather admire your *selfishness* at this point. And the blindness, pettiness, and frugality of your selfishness. For it is selfish to experience one's own judgment as a universal law; and this selfishness is blind, petty and frugal because it betrays that you have not yet discovered yourself nor created for yourself an ideal of your own, your very own—for that could never be somebody else's and much less that of all, all![14]

The qualities of the Kantian moral paradigm are a "firmness," a faith in the moral judgment, the idea that we need go no further. But Nietzsche goes on to ask whether this firmness might not merely be stubbornness. In this passage Nietzsche elaborates on another point as well. What about the insistence that our firmness be everyone else's firmness?

If our firmness were our stubbornness, then what light would it shed on our making that "value" universal? It looks self-serving. But it is not a selfishness which could be good and healthy, that is, not self-affirmation. The problem is that, as it stands, it denies that these values belong to the self. For Nietzsche, all this betrays a superficiality and unwillingness to look inward to the source of one's values. This is an unwillingness to project and stand by values which the individuals acknowledge as their own although they have created them. It is a kind of moral cowardice.

Courage is a very strong value for Nietzsche, but only certain types are valuable. He says,

> I distinguish between courage in the face of people, courage in the face of things, and courage in the face of paper .... I distinguish further between courage before witnesses and courage without witnesses: the courage of a Christian, of a believer in God in general, can never be courage without witnesses—this fact alone degrades it. I distinguish, finally, courage rooted in temperament and courage rooted in fear of fear: a particular instance of the latter type is moral courage. There should also be added courage from despair.[15]

It is impossible for Christians to act without a witness, since they believe in a God who witnesses everything. To act without witnesses is to act for only yourself and since Nietzsche wants to shift the weight of moral responsibility back to the individual, and off the shoulders of a God, he looks for a person of courage who needs neither reinforcement from a God nor praise from other people.

The parallels with Dostoyevsky are again striking. In the novella "Notes from Underground," the underground man is also struck by the willingness of most people to stop at the surface: the so-called "man of action." He also remarks on their willingness to be comforted by laws and mock certainties. In the "Grand Inquisitor" chapter of *The Brothers Karamazov*, Fyodor Dostoyevsky explores the need for communal conformity in matters of belief, in this case, in the form of worship. The killing of other people in order to have one God, in order for your God to triumph, is an example of this.

We have said that Nietzsche is interested in looking for a possible origin of contemporary European morality. The very idea of a morality having an origin presupposes a critique of the conceptions of morality discussed above. To look at these moralities as having a history is already to suggest that they are something which changes over time. Nietzsche has also given us a view of history which suggests that history is not necessarily going anywhere in particular. It is, of itself, directionless. It is not rational, not guided by any teleology, nor is it moving toward the realization of the spirit. He wants to divorce this morality from the idea that it has transcendental origins, is pre-existent, and discovered by reason (characteristics which many ethical theories presuppose). According to Nietzsche, moralities, like everything else, are invented. But they are invented in response to a concrete situation.

Nietzsche certainly is not the first to look for the origins of contemporary morality in material and cultural practices of the world. Nietzsche examines this phenomenon in the work of Paul Ree. Ree's book *Der Ursprung der moralischen Empfindungen* (The Origin of the Moral Sensations) of 1877 is mentioned in the preface to *The Genealogy of Morals*. Nietzsche describes it as a "perverse species of genealogical hypothesis, the genuinely *English* type,"[16] The "English," in the empirical tradition, were also involved in tracing the history of moral concepts. Among them, it was also believed that values originated in human activities, but the empiricist's emphasis was on need instead of creation or creative illusion. For example, they sometimes sought the origins of morality in the material needs of the species for self-preservation. The morality "still believes in good and evil and experiences the triumph of the good and the annihilation of evil as a task (that is English; typical case: the flathead John Stuart Mill); ..."[17] As a consequence, the contemporary notion of the good was still seen as arising from a positive value. This was left over from Christianity and translated into a material context.

Even though this type of morality abandons many of the things which Nietzsche finds fault with in the transcendental type of philosophy; he is still critical of it.

> These historians of morality (mostly Englishmen) do not amount to much. Usually they themselves are still quite unsuspectingly obedient to one particular morality and, without knowing it, ... Their usual mistaken premise is that they affirm some consensus of the nations, at least of tame nations, concerning certain principles of morals, and then they infer from this that these principles must be unconditionally binding also for you and me; or, conversely, they see the truth that among different nations moral valuations are *necessarily* different and then infer from this that *no* morality is at all binding. Both procedures are equally childish.[18]

In the case of these moral philosophers who, according to Nietzsche, do some things right (that is, they acknowledge that morals have a history), there is still a problem. One of the characteristics of the transcendental perspective was that it legitimated a universal order. It did this, in the case of the Christians, by the device of the story of creation, which expresses the belief that one God created all the world. But there is an analogue to this in enlightenment thought. Here we find that people preserve many of the Christian beliefs (for example the idea of equality before God) by using the idea of a reason which is in all people. The response of these British philosophers is either to continue on that quest, attempting to find universal values by empirical investigation or "they see the truth" that differing and incompatible values exist in the world and the consequence is despair.

The empiricist views retained a perspective which was not phenomenological in Nietzsche's sense; it was still non-experiential. They revolved around an idea of what was good for the species. The ends tend to be species specific and consequently to deny our personal involvement in the creation of morals. Once again, they come from outside.

> Against the theory that the isolated individual has in view the advantage of the species, of his posterity, at the cost of his own advantage: that is only an appearance.
> The tremendous importance the individual accords to the sexual

> instinct is not a result of its importance for the species, but arises because procreation is the real achievement of the individual and consequently his highest interest, his highest expression of power (not judged from the consciousness but from the center of the whole individuation).[19]

But individuals, not species, act. This way of looking at morality tends to minimize our interested perspective, hence like other forms of positivism it still is desirous of obtaining objectivity and detachment—still caught in the program of the earlier search for truth and certainty. Nietzsche does not see the relevance of a species (sub historical?) or a trans-historical perspective. He sees human motivation, at least healthy human motivation, as coming from individual, although culturally, informed, perspectives. Consider Nietzsche's remark about utilitarians, "Man does *not* strive for pleasure; only the Englishman does."[20] The empiricist account may be accurate for the origin of some moralities, but certainly not for all. Some people may have justified their moralities by such an appeal. The empiricists commit an error which is in some ways akin to that of the transcendentalists; the desire to give one explanation for all morality makes them blind to the different motivations which lie behind the many moralities we find even in Western history. They desire to have their morality triumphant.

It might be worth discussing what I take Nietzsche to mean by a morality and ethics before we get too embroiled in the details of his analysis of contemporary moral schemes. To many philosophers, the term "ethics" is what we use to designate a system of beliefs, especially one with formal structures. "Morality" often refers to a less structured view which includes the values themselves and the way they fit together in the lives of a people or person. These values tend to emphasize principles and laws the values which are "important enough" to be publicly declared. I take Nietzsche to be looking at "morality" in most of his writings in an even broader sense than the one we are accustomed to: one which includes the customs and mores of a people—not merely their principles and laws. We have, actually, already seen examples of Nietzsche using this broader conception. He explains how momentous our small, seemingly inconsequential, actions are. In the following chapter, we will find this issue of the breadth of value discussed again in an aesthetic context. Nietzsche used it earlier in this analysis when he talked about the consequence to valuation of the death of God (Chapter 1, "Madman"). In these passages he suggested that we have to go beyond looking at the obvious consequences of a collapse of the structure of belief.

Let us for a moment reconsider the traditional example from the same context (that is the Christian moral scheme). If God is dead, we must go beyond the fact that the ten commandments no longer have force as commandments, to look at the other customs and practices which will have to change. These things are so much a part of the fabric of our lives that they have become invisible. It is also true that their ties to the historical development of Christianity are no longer visible. They seem, instead, to be facts which are part of our moral world. All of these are, however, morally relevant. They are parts of our reality and, as

Nietzsche suggests in the section called "Little Deviant Acts" (Chapter 1), not insignificant parts! This is why Nietzsche chides the atheist as much as the believer for not going beyond Christian morality. As we have seen, he construes morality in a very wide sense and ties it in with various types of social and cultural practices embedded in our history.

Nietzsche is not concerned with simply giving a history of the origin of contemporary European morality. He says:

> I see nobody who ventured a *critique* of moral valuations; I miss even the slightest attempts of scientific curiosity, of the refined, experimental imagination of psychologists and historians that readily anticipates a problem and catches it in flight without quite knowing what it has caught. I have scarcely detected a few meager preliminary efforts to explore the *history of the origins* of these feelings and valuations (which is something quite different from a critique and again different from a history of ethical systems).[21]

A critique is needed: One which touches us in a deep personal way, where we live. "All great problems demand great love" Nietzsche says in the same section. They demand a passion—someone who will approach "this problem as his own personal distress, torment, voluptuousness, and passion...."

According to Nietzsche "we need a critique of all moral values; the intrinsic worth of these values must, first of all be called in question."[22] In *On the Genealogy of Morals*, a text which uses the etymologies to assist in the historical understanding of certain moral categories, Nietzsche says:

> A certain amount of historical and philological training, together with a native fastidiousness in matters of psychology, before long transformed this problem [his youthful toying with the problem of evil] to another, to wit, "Under what conditions did man construct the value judgments *good* and *evil* "? And what is their intrinsic worth? Have they thus far benefited or retarded mankind?[23]

The critique begins with a look at certain values. Nietzsche uses the tools he has, in this case those of the historian and philologist, to assist him in his task. He wants to know what human conditions gave birth to the values good and evil, and whether they enhance or diminish the joys and sorrows of our lives. Nietzsche sees himself as asking a different kind of question about morality, a question which begins by looking into the origins of a value scheme. In the course of his search for the origin of our contemporary moral concepts, Nietzsche discovers two kinds of "morality": master and slave morality. These two moralities are distinguished by the differing perspectives of the group of people who create them. And they are found in both European and antique societies, which is not to say that they are transcendental principles.[24]

My interpretation is designed to show that all values come from a culturally informed yet individually experienced perspective. All values are human creations. Human existence and living is necessarily bound to a perspective. A value scheme cannot be evaluated from a perspectively privileged position. This connection explains Nietzsche's belief that the search for the value of ethics must lead one to consider questions about the origin of ethical systems. Nietzsche says, "this origin mattered to me only as one of the means toward an end. The end was the *value* of ethics ...."[25]

Morality has its origins in human practice. The search for these origins is a prerequisite to evaluation. The perspective which informed the original creation of values will be relevant in the current reevaluation of a practice. This is not the same as saying that the origin of a practice will determine the outcome of the evaluation. "Even if a morality has grown out of an error, the realization of this fact would not as much as touch the problem of its value."[26] The point is not that value should be divorced from context and not vulnerable to contextual criticisms; it is, rather, that its value must yet be questioned in the contemporary context. It is in this context that we must make judgments about its worth. Nietzsche continues: "Thus nobody up to now has examined the *value* of that most famous of all medicines which is called morality; and the first step would be—for once to *question it*. Well then, precisely this is our task."[27]

Nietzsche is, in this characterization of what is morally relevant to evaluation, attacking the conception of morality of which we have spoken earlier. We can call it "objective." In contrast to this, the acknowledgment of the enrootedness of values is what is material in Nietzsche's contribution to moral evaluation. Practices and values will be better evaluated when we consider them in the context in which they were created, and not, as was supposed by the objectivist, when we see them without a context, in isolation or "in themselves." The thought that we might take a moral action and evaluate it apart from considering the people who perform it and the context within which it occurred seems entirely ridiculous to Nietzsche. The identity of the people is vital because of their life history and place in the social matrix. This will become more obvious in the following discussion of the "moralities."

As I mentioned earlier, the master and slave moralities are distinguished by their perspectives. And they reflect the place they each hold in a power relation. Nietzsche is not terribly interested in the actual historical origin of the power relation, nor in categorizing the type of power, but rather in the psychological and philosophical effects of being in and out of power. By psychological and philosophical, I mean effects on attitude and thought, respectively. These form the basis for the plausibility of the alternative historical account Nietzsche is offering. Since, class, situation, and psychological type determine perspective, Nietzsche chose historical periods where there were major differences in these categories to illustrate his analysis.

Master Morality or "*Herren/Moral*"[28] is represented by a number of historical types: "Roman," "pagan," "classical," "Renaissance."[29] This gives us a sense of the psychological type he is talking about. In the broader historical example Nietzsche is thinking of a type of morality which predated Christianity. In any event, he takes the master morality to be an earlier type of morality. The masters are the creators of the good and see themselves as such. According to them, "I am good and therefore what issues from me is good." It is in seeing themselves as good that the masters make their first and primary moral distinction. This is not something we get the impression they reflect upon, but it is something which they unconsciously create. Morality from the master's perspective is largely a matter of the masters exercising their will and bringing about the fulfillment of their desire. Morality is a matter of action, in a positive sense, that is, embracing something as a value and acting on that value. This is not a morality which focuses on constraining action nor on evaluating actions according to a prescribed social norm.

Morality in this case is primarily a matter of determining values, of creation. It is not a matter of evaluating actions.

> What is noble? ... It is not actions that prove him—actions are always open to many interpretations, always unfathomable —nor is it "works".... It is not the works, it is the *faith* that is decisive here, that determines the order of rank.... The *noble soul has reverence for itself.*[30]

Being moral is not something the masters do because they are compelled whether by law, conscience, or principle, but rather something done because they are noble and proud. Their code of ethics, with respect to actions affecting other people, will depend upon those people's relation to them and the master's view of themselves. The code is in no way universal; if it was, that would include the masters in the ranks of those whom they are unlike and have no desire to be like. In *Beyond Good and Evil* Nietzsche writes: "Signs of nobility: never thinking of degrading our duties into duties for everybody; not wanting to delegate, to share, one's own responsibility; counting one's privileges and their exercise among one's *duties*."[31] These ways of behaving, these duties, do not come about in response to some higher law, they are matters of good taste. Self-respect or mutual respect, instead of obedience to some higher law, is what governs the master's treatment of their peers.

A group of people remains who are not peers, a group which good taste demands be excluded from the respect owed to those who value themselves. These are the slaves. The "other" of the master morality is noticed, if at all, with an attitude bordering on indifference. The slaves are bad because they are not masters. What they are, to the master, is primarily negative: not honest, not proud, in short, not noble. The power relations between master and slave preclude or make unnecessary a more exhaustive examination of the slave's nature. After all, of what concern is it to the master?

"Good" and "bad" are the moral designations which characterize the master morality. The main emphasis is on the one who has power: the master. The good comes from a feeling of self-respect, of self-mastery. The designation bad, coming also from the master, is the voice of exclusion. It says "they" are not our type. Hence the impossibility of universality in a master morality. From the master's point of view, a universal morality would hardly be a desirable option.[32] It would include the masters in a class of people with whom they could have had no desire to be classed. Nietzsche says, "The origin of the opposites good and bad is to be found in the pathos of nobility and distance, representing the dominant temper of a higher, ruling class in relation to a lower, dependent one."[33]

In looking at the origin of both moralities Nietzsche is giving us an analysis of a particular cultural phenomenon. He has said that the master morality is an earlier one. He means this in terms of its cultural predominance; the master morality ruled the antique world until the advent of Christianity. The slave morality also has its roots in the ancient cultures which produced the master morality, but it had quite different antecedents (Heraclitus vs. Parmenides, Sophocles vs. Euripides). These moralities can be viewed in another, more psychological, way. They can be looked at as showing the cultural projection of values which are imbedded in one relation (that between the master and the slave), looked at from differing points of view. Nietzsche is doing both. He is both looking at the points of view in the power relation and looking at these moralities as representing historical types. In the case of the slave morality we find quite different moral designations: "good" and "evil." We should note how different this is from the master moralities "good" and "bad." It is not only that "bad" changes to "evil" but the "good" changes dramatically as well.

The slave morality or "*Sklaven/Moral*,"[34] as Nietzsche puts it, also focuses on the masters. The masters are considered evil because they have power. From the slave's point of view the master wields that power in an arbitrary, a capricious manner. Slaves do not and cannot see the motivations which are a part of the world of the masters, a world from which they are excluded. The slaves have reason to doubt the "goods" of the master. They are "goods" which exclude or harm the slaves. The goods of the slaves are not ones which merely embellish life: they are rather those which make life possible or less horrible. Nietzsche says, "suppose the violated, oppressed, suffering, unfree, who are uncertain of themselves moralize"; from their perspective the most natural reaction would be a pessimism about life.[35] The slaves are involved with the narrowly utilitarian concerns of life, not because they want to be, but because they must.

In *The Mill on the Floss*, George Eliot gives a delightful illustration of the way our point of view colors our perceptions of people's lives and values. Like Nietzsche, she is interested in considering how the perspective which grows out of the way we live informs our views of what is right and what is wrong. She uses the example of a pike and a roach.

> ... a pike and a roach can [not] look at each other from a similar point of view. The roach necessarily abhors the mode in which the pike gets his living, and the pike is likely to think nothing further of even the most indignant roach than that he is excellent good eating; it could only be when the roach choked him that the pike could entertain a strong personal animosity.[36]

The roach cannot even choke the pike at will and therefore can never *demand* the kind of attention from it which would begin to mitigate its indignation. The roach and the slave are in the unhappy position of having no or little influence over the being who decides their fate. They simply do not matter; and what is worse, they know they do not.

The masters have power, the masters create themselves, and create the noble morality. The slaves are in no position to seize power openly. They must resort to subterfuge if they are to affect their will on the world and so they lie, work through others, and manipulate. This is a mark of their strength, of their will to power, not merely their weakness. It shows they are not broken. The slaves are forced to be clever, and shrewd in a way which is not straightforward. Nietzsche says of the slave:

> A race of such men will, in the end, inevitably be cleverer than a race of aristocrats, and it will honor sharp-wittedness to a much greater degree, i.e., as an absolutely vital condition for its existence.[37]

Their intellectual development will not be encouraged to pursue education and refinement of the type allotted to the masters. They will be forced by their circumstances to learn from experience and from other slaves. They will have to rely upon each other for comfort, and to this underground philosophy Christianity which contains a new moral justification. This can be seen in the above passages and by considering the herd-like mentality which Nietzsche attributes to the Christians.

In both of these cases, the focus of the morality is on the powerful. In each case, this is originally the master. But, being able to define a situation is a powerful device. When the slave redefines morality and the masters begin to fear that there might be some truth in this new definition, there is a shift in power—a shift in favor of the slave.

Nietzsche gives us an insightful analysis of the history of European culture. He undermines the view of morality and moral values as being perspectiveless. His analysis admits the possibility of various perspectives with varying claims to legitimacy. He acknowledges the possibility of both revision and moral revolution. The analysis itself provides direction for the process of re-evaluation.

Nietzsche does mean to be a radical and a revolutionary, even to a certain extent a liberator, but he is also a radical aristocrat. Emma Goldman reporting a conversation, says, "I pointed out that Nietzsche was not a social theorist but a poet, rebel, and innovator. His aristocracy was neither of birth nor of purse; it was of the spirit. In that respect Nietzsche was an anarchist, and all true anarchists were aristocrats."[38] He created a new notion of an elite, one to which he would have access.

Let us remember that the two moralities we have considered so far do not merely represent two perspectives on the same situations. They also are meant to represent the changing historical situation as it is writ large on European culture. Contemporary culture has responded to pressure from the slave, and the result is a morality which is the dominant cultural force: Christianity. But Nietzsche now recommends that morality go beyond good and evil. He believes that the modern world should reject the slave morality, especially as it is embodied in the Christian ethic whose alleged values are meekness, humility, and selflessness. Its condemnation of self-respect, the emphasis on laws or rules which require obedience, the subjugation to a "higher" authority are all part of a morality which results in pessimism. This pessimism is of the type which negates the values which are a part of this world, the world we live in and perceive. What we need, by contrast, is a morality which affirms life, this life.

Some of the features of the master morality were life affirming. Now, having done his genealogy of morals, Nietzsche can go back and look at the values which were a part of other moralities. According to Nietzsche, the master morality did affirm life. The masters had every reason to affirm their life: it was good. This straightforward valuation is part of what Nietzsche admires in these "barbarians." Their morality was healthy because it flowed from their almost simpleminded feelings about themselves and what they did. This mental health is largely a result of the unchallenged experience of being powerful. It is the opposite of the rancorous, self-denying Christian morality which is the consequence of the powerless and hopeless situation of the slave.

> The slave revolt in morals begins by rancor turning creative and giving birth to values—the rancor of beings who, deprived of the direct outlet of action, compensate by an imaginary vengeance. All truly noble morality grows out of triumphant self-affirmation.[39]

Self-affirmation will be one of the most striking features of Nietzsche's conception of moral, and spiritual health.

Nietzsche is not recommending a return to the master morality, but many of his suggestions for a new morality do have an affinity with the perspective of the "noble," if not the "barbarian." Nietzsche wants the new morality to come from value creators who acknowledge themselves as such. In other words, they need appeal to nothing "higher," more universal than their own desire or will. This is a result of being of this world and concerned with this world.

> In the narrower sphere of so-called moral values one cannot find a greater contrast than that between a *master morality* and the morality of *Christian* value concepts: the latter developed on soil that was morbid through and through ..., master morality ... is, conversely, the sign language of what has turned out well, of *ascending* life, of the will to power as the principle of life. Master morality *affirms* as instinctively as Christian morality *negates* .... The former gives to things out of its own abundance—it transfigures, it beautifies the world and *makes it more rational (vernünftigt)*—the latter impoverishes, pales and makes uglier the value of things, it

negates the world. "World" is a Christian term of abuse.[40]

Nietzsche is trying to show that the noble morality respects things of this world. The affirmation of life is one of the features a "healthy" new morality will have.

The new morality will go beyond because it comes from beings who are creators instead of merely destroyers. We cannot say exactly where they will go. In Nietzsche's book *Zarathustra* the prophet of the *Übermensch* says, "And verily, I love you for not knowing how to live today, you higher men! For thus *you* live best."[41] Not knowing how to live is the right response to the situation the higher person is in! There is no simple correct response to the world and there is no formula for acting correctly. We must accept this when we accept the transitory nature of this world.

The health and simple straight-forwardness of the master was undermined in the inversion of values which came about when the slave morality was in ascendance: during the Christian period. Slave values of collectivity, industriousness, and equality were turned on the masters with the result that the master's confidence and simple honesty were undermined. They began to doubt themselves. Naturally their conduct, which was largely indifferent to others, especially to the lowly and meek, did not fare well under the judgment of people whose values were the inverse of theirs. According to Nietzsche, in this period the masters lost many of those good traits they had had. Under Christianity they become self-conscious, timid, in short, no longer masterly.

The masters are now in an unhappy, unhealthy position. They have to think about the meaning of their action to others—specifically how they will be judged. They have to think about consequences. They must feel vulnerable to retribution. All this is a consequence of the creation of that other world. In eternity, according to the slave, all the wrongs will be righted. These wrongs are those perpetrated on the slaves.

Let us consider the following passage from *The Case of Wagner*.

> Noble morality, master morality, conversely, is rooted in a triumphant Yes said to *oneself*—it is self-affirmation, self-glorification of life; it also requires sublime symbols and practices, but only because "its heart is too full." All of *beautiful*, all of *great* art belongs here: the essence of both is gratitude.[42]

The people who are representatives of the master morality are not necessarily unconcerned with others. This is true in spite of the fact that the most elemental characteristic of their morality is this "Yes said to *oneself*." The nature of the concern is what is at issue. The masters are not concerned with other people because of guilt or bad conscience which would taint their actions with self-serving altruism—altruism which aims at making the giver feel superior. Instead, the noble person acts in a true spirit of generosity because "its heart is too full." These are aspects of the "morality" which Nietzsche wants to preserve.

The slaves, on the other hand, accepted the lie which justified the conditions of their life, the myth of another world. This "other world" represents for Nietzsche the whole series of metaphysical problems which have been discussed earlier. This is a problem the culture is only beginning to get itself out of because it has only taken the first step: recognizing the death of God. Nietzsche is trying to push us toward a purge which is so much greater in extent; the rooting out of those values and beliefs still a part of this now discredited point of view. This is the unhappy and problematic situation from which the higher person must emerge. Nietzsche recommends that the slave values which are the result of rancor and a desire for vengeance be eliminated from our culture by a radical re-evaluation of all values. But we must also eliminate the world which their hatred created.

Nietzsche feels a certain natural repugnance toward the slave and the representatives of the slave morality in Europe. He feels this toward all egalitarian thinkers whether they are democrats, communists, or utilitarians. So it is not only the Christian morality of which he is critical: any morality which does away with differentiation and proposes to treat people equally is suspect. Nietzsche is as critical of judging in general as he is of this emphasis on equality before a judge. Part of his criticism is that many of these moral or political systems are motivated by pity and concern for others. He is contemptuous of those who allow themselves to be brought down in this way. We should not lower ourselves to the condition of the slave. "The higher must not be made an instrument of the lower: the 'pathos of distance' must to all eternity keep separate tasks separate."[43] The higher people and the *Übermenschen* cannot involve themselves in the abstract notions of equality which are part of the life negating values of philosophers like Plato, Protagoras, and Parmenides. But Kantian morality is still Nietzsche's prime target.

> Anyone who still judges "in this case everybody would have to act like this" has not yet taken five steps toward self-knowledge. Otherwise he would know that there neither are nor can be actions that are the same; that every action that has ever been done was done in an altogether unique and irretrievable way, and that this will be equally true of every future action; that all regulations [*Vorschriften*] about actions relate only to their coarse exterior (even the most inward and subtle regulations of all moralities so far); that these regulations may lead to some semblance of sameness, but *really only to some semblance; ...*[44]

Nietzsche believes that the morality of treating equal actions equally is an extension of the notion of equality of persons. If we treat actions the same no matter who performed them, then we ignore the real differences between actions. In separating the doer from the deed, we remove something which is potentially relevant to the evaluation. In doing this, we ignore the uniqueness of motivation and situation which are a part of all activities.

As a result of his reevaluation of values Nietzsche has found reason, he feels, to reinstate some of the master values. Many conditions which naturally result from being empowered are healthy and good. Nietzsche is attracted to another aspect of that world and set of values, to the idea of moral agent as warrior, a kind of lonely hero creating a world out of chaos and vice. The ends of this person are not world mastery, but rather self-mastery. Yet Nietzsche sees self-mastery arising out of conflict and contest (if not conquest). The warriors need noble enemies, this ennobles them, it helps them to challenge themselves and therefore to go beyond themselves. The world seems to exist for the sake of their ego—to stimulate them, provoke them, to make them better. It allows them to realize their independence. This is in marked contrast to the condition and perspective of the slave.

> Conversely the need for faith, for some kind of unconditional Yes and No, ... is a need born of *weakness*. The man of faith the "believer" of every kind, is necessarily a dependent man—one who cannot posit *himself* as an end, one who cannot posit any end at all by himself.[45]

The slaves liked nothing better than to have their decisions made for them so that they need only believe. Again, this is similar to the way the masses of people are characterized in the "Grand Inquisitor" passage of *The Brothers Karamazov* by Dostoyevsky. The Grand Inquisitor's argument is based on the realization that the majority of human beings want to hand over the responsibility of moral creation to an authority outside of themselves. In contrast, the *Übermenschen* are constantly involved in positing themselves. They posit themselves against enemies, against friends, but also they posit themselves as an end which does not require anything to be against. They posit themselves as a possibility into the future.

Nietzsche's final view is of a morality which emphasizes an individual's involved phenomenological perspective. A morality which will respond to the varying historical and social conditions: the power relations in society. Commentators on Nietzsche's work in the past, for example, Goldman, Hamilton, Kaufmann, and Brinton, have emphasized Nietzsche's morality of the individual as it has been represented here. I want to show that the emphasis on the individual is not simply aimed at giving us a heroic individual battling against the herd. Nietzsche is a far more complex and interesting thinker than that interpretation would lead one to believe. Nietzsche's point is a philosophical one. By getting us to look at the morality from the point of view of the individual, he gets us to abandon the perspective of a judge. The judge's is the perspective which he believes has dominated the Western view of morality and Western philosophy. He wants us to look at morality from the point of view of an individual living in society. This gets us to change our relation to our own morality.

Nietzsche's *Übermenschen* are not enslavers of human beings, not nationalists, although perhaps they are sexists, and racists. They are individuals who may act out of compassion but will not be compelled from pity. Their self-mastery does not require or even recommend mastery over another. The struggle of the *Übermenschen* is not an attempt to enslave or humiliate an inferior; like the pikes mentioned earlier, they will be indifferent to those who do not have power or are not equal to them. If they are not indifferent, they can be helpful or generous from a sense of there own overfullness. This is quite different from pity.

Nietzsche's beyond good and evil morality is predicated upon discrimination and hierarchy. The *Übermenschen* are superior beings. But they do not represent a class nor do they necessarily come out of some particular class or tradition. However, we should remember that, as Nietzsche mentions above, whatever the intentions, the perceived reality; the view of the people on the bottom of the hierarchy is another and equally legitimate way of seeing the situation. Remember what the masters looked like from the slaves' point of view.

> ... anyone who knew these "good" ones only as enemies would find them evil enemies indeed. For these same men who, amongst themselves, are so strictly constrained by custom, worship, ritual, gratitude, and by mutual surveillance and jealousy, who are so resourceful in consideration, tenderness, loyalty, pride, and friendship, when once they step outside their circle become little better than uncaged beasts of prey. Once abroad in the wilderness, they revel in the freedom from social constraint and compensate for their long confinement in the quietude of their own community. They revert to the innocence of wild animals: we can imagine them returning from an orgy of murder, arson, rape, and torture, jubilant and at peace with themselves ....[46]

Because the new morality retains so many elements of the master morality's perspective, it imitates the exclusionary practices of the master morality. Like the master, constrained at home but totally at liberty abroad. the new morality continues to create an "other," a group of people about whom the masters have no concern. Many commentators have found this a worrisome aspect of Nietzsche's morality. Kaufmann, Hollingdale, and Brinton express this fear, although Kaufmann tries to counter it with a more measured account. But there is something appropriate about this desire to get beyond a preoccupation with what other people are doing. This is true in at least two senses. One is the preoccupation with judging other people and watching them. The other is the more positive desire to affirm one's self, rather than to be always worrying about someone else or how one's actions will be perceived.

> *Private morality, world morality.* Since man no longer believes that a God is guiding the destinies of the world as a whole, or that, despite all apparent twists, the path of mankind is leading somewhere glorious, men must set themselves ecumenical goals, embracing the whole earth. The older

> morality, namely Kant's, demands from the individual those actions that one desires from all men—a nice, a naive idea, as if everyone without further ado would know which manner of action would benefit the whole of mankind, that is, which actions were desirable at all .... In any event, if mankind is to keep from destroying itself ... we must discover first a *knowledge of the conditions of culture*, a knowledge surpassing all previous knowledge, as a scientific [*wissenschaftlicher*] standard for ecumenical goals. This is the enormous task of the great minds [*Geister*] of the next century.[47]

At the beginning of our discussion of ethics in this chapter,[48] I talked about a view of morality which Nietzsche finds unattractive. It is a part of the slavish morality which, although it did not originate there, is still exemplified in the work of Kant. This model of morality was one where the individuals judged a situation by proposing a maxim and evaluating it according to a rule or law. They came to a conclusion about the right thing to do, and then considered this judgment to be binding on them with respect to their actions. Thus, acting "good" had to do with acting in conformity with law: either moral law or the Christian God's law.

Nietzsche believes that everything is wrong with this model of morality. Specifically, the definition of morality as obedience to a law is wrong in two ways. First, it acknowledges that there exist moral laws: Nothing about morality, in Nietzsche's view, is lawlike. Second, it requires obedience to something outside of itself and something higher than itself. In this it betrays its slavish origins. The model of good action, in this case, is doing what someone else has determined to be good. The condition of the slave allowed no more than this. Nietzsche, on the other hand, demands much more than this from a "moral" being. He demands the creation of values within the social and cultural setting. This is both the task of an individual and that of a culture. The model for value creation is a model which takes its original from the activities of an artist. We will examine that model and the example of the creative artist in more detail in the following Chapter. Before going on to this let us look at his remarks on moral judgment in *The Gay Science*.

> Let us therefore *limit* ourselves to the purification of our opinions and valuations and to the *creation of our own new tables of what is good*, and let us stop brooding about the "moral value of our actions!" Yes, my friends, regarding all the moral chatter of some about others it is time to feel nauseous. Sitting in moral judgment should offend our taste.[49]

Nietzsche wants us to abandon the view of morality which gets its value from the fact that its value judgments are "higher" than those of our culture or ourselves.' The "moral value of our actions" was to be determined against a standard. That standard and its worth were determined by the fact that they were judged by beings superior in some way; priests, or gods, or philosophers. The emphasis on judgment in evaluation, instead of giving value, is what should disgust us. The preoccupation of some people with the moral values of others betrays their lack of security in their own values. They need communal conformity in their belief to make it believable even to themselves. The idea that moralities should be policed comes from a culture which is preoccupied with passing judgment.

"Sitting in moral judgment should offend our taste." Nietzsche is not just saying that we should experience aesthetic or stylistic revulsion to this model of morality. This is a strong statement coming from Nietzsche. Our taste is part of who we are, it gives color to existence. It sets the stamp of our personalities on our actions. Nietzsche finds something distasteful about "sitting in judgment." This offense extends to the judges and their petty interest in evaluating someone else's actions. It offends Nietzsche's taste. A kind of voyeurism motivates such an interest. We must link this view with Nietzsche's remarks on courage. God stands behind the Christians' actions to give them "courage" so that they are not alone. This is not courage, according to Nietzsche. The Christian God is the ultimate voyeur because nothing is unknown or unseen. But Nietzsche distrusts human actions which have to be backed up or bolstered by such an authority. Judgment is the activity of the God of the Old Testament, and we also see the Christian of the New Testament is waiting for judgment. These two facts alone should make us suspicious.

Nietzsche's critique of philosophy attempted to eliminate this perspective and all that imitated it, whether consciously or unconsciously. Most Western morality has adopted the perspective of a judge (or at least the perspective of a removed spectator, in the case of the empiricisms mentioned earlier). The model for the "fair" passing of judgment in the moral and political context of contemporary culture is one where the judges are uninvolved in the situation about which they must judge. Even the real involvement of being the judge is unemphasized. The laws to which the judge has reference, whether they are the ten commandments, or statutes are brought down to the particular in the act of judging. This is only to say they are interpreted. But their strength is seen to lie in their universality and emptiness of the value. Morality on a Christian model prioritizes the spectator's point of view, the view of the judge of the person outside of the experience or situation. A standard exists for what is good, and the individual or action is judged according to conformity with the standard.

Nietzsche has no quarrel with the activity of judging or what he calls evaluation. It is not that he wants us to refrain from judging in that sense. But he is objecting to fixed standards and claims of impartiality which are part of a certain view of the valuable judge. Perhaps, instead of obscuring interest and biases, it would be more helpful to have them in the open so that we could tell if something were judged "fairly." The fairness would then have to do with a type of honesty which reveals motivation. The advantage would be to the constant revision which value and truth undergo. A thing's value or truth is not decided once and for all. So the motivation for a judgment, far from being irrelevant, can assist in the later process.

Not much has been said of morality or judging in a political context, because that does not seem to be Nietzsche's primary interest. He is interested in the social and cultural meaning of actions, especially in the way they are attached to their origins. But he is perhaps more interested in the way individuals perceive themselves and each other. This perceiving each other is not meant in the voyeuristic sense mentioned above, not with the intent of passing judgment, but to see each other as models or examples of lives. Rather than passing judgment on someone's life from our own set of values or from some cultural standard, we can evaluate by going outside of ourselves into their world. Simone de Beauvoir seems to be suggesting this when she says of her relationship to Jean-Paul Sartre, "But Sartre always tried to see me as part of my own set of values and attitudes."[50] Here was evaluation which was not preoccupied with passing judgment. The evaluation takes place in the context of values which de Beauvoir herself has created. If Sartre really looked at her in the context of her beliefs and to allow their legitimacy, then this is something like what I think Nietzsche has in mind.

Such evaluation must not be mistaken for a doctrine of tolerance, because it is anything but that. First, it is not applied democratically. Nietzsche is himself obviously quite intolerant of many beliefs, people, and their views. And, although consistency is not his strong point, a lack of hypocrisy is. It is not tolerance which makes for this gentle attitude, but I think something like a desire to learn, to be carried on beyond the relatively narrow version of our own right and wrong, of good and bad, of what offends our taste and what enhances it. The point of this going beyond is twofold. We both acknowledge the fact that we are moving in history with no knowledge of where we will end up (but with *some* control over it), and we consider values besides our own, which can be models for our own future actions.

Chapter Three

AESTHETICS AND THE SWITCH FROM THE PERSPECTIVE OF A JUDGE TO THAT OF A PARTICIPANT

> *What one should learn from artists.*—How can we make things beautiful, attractive, and desirable for us when they are not? And I rather think that in themselves they never are ... artists [who] are really continually trying to bring off such inventions and feats. Moving away from things until there is a good deal that one no longer sees and there is much that our eye has to add if we are still to see them at all; or seeing things around a corner and as cut out and framed; or to place them so that they partially conceal each other and grant us only glimpses of architectural perspectives; or looking at them through tinted glass or in the light of the sunset; or giving them a surface and skin that is not fully transparent—all this we should learn from artists while being wiser than they are in other matters. For with them this subtle power usually comes to an end where art ends and life begins; but we want to be the poets of our life—first of all in the smallest, most everyday matters.[1]

In this chapter, I will discuss the importance of aesthetic theory and value in Nietzsche's philosophy. He uses his understanding of the difference between the creation and appreciation of aesthetic value as a model for understanding his version of morality (post-Christian morality or value-making beyond good and evil) and moralities in general (those of the past). In Chapter One and Chapter Two, I explored some of the vestiges of other-worldly perspectives which we still find in contemporary philosophical theories and practices. I looked at Nietzsche's critiques and recommendations concerning philosophical methodology and moral values. In both cases there was an other-worldly model of knowing and valuing which Nietzsche did not believe withstood his critique. In this third chapter, I will look at a variety of perspectives on art. Not all of these are other-worldly, but they represent a shift in perspective which matters as much in this context as the other was in its context. Nietzsche will continue his critique of these types of perspective. Then I will look at what he recommends to take their place.

I will explore the way he uses the genealogical method which we have already seen him advocate. He will use this method of examination and evaluation in a new philosophical area: aesthetics. As we have seen, two serious consequences follow from this: Nietzsche will show that, in their writings on aesthetics, many philosophers have made the same "error" as they have in the areas of philosophy. He will look at art from a different perspective, one which escapes those errors. This anticipates what he will do in the case of morality. Hints of this were seen in the second chapter. The same critique which was offered in the case of all transcendental philosophies will be offered in the case of the aesthetic philosopher. It will then be used to criticize the view of art which is obsessed with passing judgment, that is, obsessed with the critic's point of view. Nietzsche believes that he will find out some things which will be useful in helping him make visible what is wrong with contemporary morality. He will do this by looking at both art and morality in this new way and by seeing the results of approaching it from these varied perspectives. In choosing this approach, I do not mean to discount Nietzsche's views on art. Nietzsche's aesthetic views stand on their own and merit careful consideration. But for now, my purpose in looking at these observations is to aid us in an examination of the similarities between art and morality, and aesthetic and moral change.

In the previous chapter, we saw that Nietzsche found remnants of other-worldliness in our penchant for looking at morality from the perspective of the judge or critic. This perspective is suspect, because it was created in imitation of that of the Christian God. It is historically and theoretically tied to what he hopes is now a discredited point of view. In the example of artistic creation (which we will now examine), an alternative is suggested to the other-worldly perspective of the moralist and judge. The perspective of the artist is one which acknowledges the involvement of the knower or doer. The model is of an artist engaged in an act of creation. The artist is attached to the world, especially attached to the "world of appearance," as it is called, because the task of the artist is to assist becoming. The task of the artist involves both creation and the sensual elements of life and experience. The fact that both these activities and aspects of aesthetic experience take place over time cannot be ignored. If we demand that philosophy make sense of these human activities, then we will need a philosophy which acknowledges both change and history in creation.

But the artist's is not the only perspective Nietzsche endorses. We have also the examples of "good" critics. These are critics who are not merely interested in passing judgment. They are interested in being responsive to a work, in helping other people to see something in it, being open to it, letting it affect them. This is opposed to the critic or judge who would rather put the work into a previously formulated structure for analysis and find out whether it passes a test. The aesthetic of the "good" critic follows the model of ethical analysis which we found in Nietzsche's view of Kant.

Let us return to Nietzsche's own analysis of art and aesthetic evaluation. He has observed some of the same tendencies in traditional philosophies of art as we found in metaphysics. These tendencies correspond with an idea of morality as implying passing judgment or passing sentence. In aesthetic philosophy many attempts are made to find a transcendental justification for art. These attempts take us outside of the lived world, and certainly outside of the culture and away from the place of the artists in that culture: their effect is to remove the artist from his or her context. They have the same unhappy consequences for art as Nietzsche found in morality, when this shift was found in that area.

A romantic view of artistic creation is complementary to this removal. This is the view of the artist as a genius or as inspired. The importance of the idea of inspiration in this context is that it assigned the honor or credit for the idea of the artwork to a god or spirit.[2] This model for understanding artistic and other creations is present in many of the world views which the West has entertained (especially those which deny the importance of history and change). It seems that it was difficult to explain creativity, which involves change and "becoming." Explaining the activity of the artist (in a system which does not provide an adequate understanding of creativity) is a problem. The effect of this type of view is to suggest that what the artists do is not their own doing. Their creations need not then be attributed to human activity or context. The problem is especially with creative activity; that is, that which produces something new within a material or phenomenological context.

An analogous problem can be found in the history of science. Our culture wants to emphasize the innovator here as well. But modern science conceives of the natural world in terms of its intelligibility—like the world of traditional philosophy. The trouble with innovation in this context is, that because the nature of that world is fixed, it must be understood in terms of discovery instead of invention. The history of science is de-emphasized and the results of inquiry (for example, laws) are emphasized. Yet, we find that same romance about the scientist that we felt about the artist. We like to look at that inspired or creative person.

Nietzsche is attracted to the arts precisely because of the difficult and ambiguous place which they occupy within philosophical thinking. The artist provides a model for living in the world and a model for Nietzsche's understanding of the phenomenon which we now call morality.

Nietzsche says, "Our aesthetics hitherto has been a woman's aesthetics to the extent that only the receivers of art have formulated their experience of 'what is beautiful?' In all philosophy hitherto the artist is lacking."[3] The male or female metaphor is used throughout this section. The idea is that women are receptacles. This is obviously borrowed from his understanding of women in a sexual context (conceived of biologically instead of experientially). The analogy does not hold up well if one has a sophisticated view of sexuality, but Nietzsche means that women "should receive," they are not in on the activity.

What Nietzsche means is that the perspective of the artist has been missing, in the way we look at the world. Instead, we adopt the perspective of a critic. We ought to try not to think in terms of the way a critic or spectator does, not from the view of one who receives and perceives; but rather in terms of one who creates. As a consequence of this missing perspective, the narrowness and inadequacy of some attempts to philosophize come to the fore. This is especially true in discussions on art. The philosophers are unable to have a sensible context for understanding creation because they already lack one for change and history. Perhaps this is why so many thinkers have been wary of art. This is especially true of Jewish and Christian thinkers who view art with distrust.[4] One often finds, coupled with this distrust, awe with respect to its power. We find this suspicion and fear toward classical authors, as well.

Plato and Aristotle exhibited a concern with art or poesis (although their judgments as to its value were different) because of its effects.[5] Leo Tolstoy did, as well.[6] Art's sensual nature and emotional effects were subjected to a careful scrutiny. These thinkers attempted to deal with that sensual element by subsuming it under the auspices of morality and religion or, as in the case of Aristotle, morality and psychological health. For Plato, various types of art were considered harmful or suspect because they were tied to deception or semblance.[7] A picture puts before us an image which is not present as if it were present, a piece of music evokes feelings which vie with our reason for control of our soul. For reasons like these, Plato recommends a strict political control over art and its uses in his ideal culture. Aristotle in the *Poetics*,[8] when he considers poetic narrative, is also concerned with its pathetic influence on the spectator. In both of these cases, the main emphasis of the treatment is on the spectator and the effects of the work. The effects are evaluated morally and politically in terms of the consequences for society or for the individual's health. Although Aristotle and Plato rule differently about the desirability of poesis, they are alike in their adoption of the perspective of a spectator in their evaluation. And this, from Nietzsche's point of view, is what is relevant.

Nietzsche criticizes philosophers' works on art in two ways. The first is that their anti-sensual prejudice (which we discussed in the previous Chapter) gets in the way. The second is that they continue in their habit of adopting the perspective of a judge (one who is removed from the process of creation): they are concerned with art's moral or political effects. Both methods are present in the work of Plato; only the judgment perspective is present in the work of Aristotle.

Nietzsche considers and discusses sensual and cultural elements in his own work. He finds these equally vital to all aspects of life, including the acquisition of knowledge. We must become suspicious when a philosopher cannot talk intelligently about art, a topic so vital to human interests and activities. We must wonder, when meaning and truth are limited to such strict "scientific" senses that even the most obvious value discriminations are unintelligible, according to them. Nietzsche believes that this betrays a hatred or fear (on the part of the philosophers) of those elements of life not so easily controlled or defined. "Thus did Plato flee from reality and desire to see things only in pallid mental pictures [forms]; he was full of sensibility and knew how easily the waves of his sensibility could close over his reason."[9] Plato was afraid of the power of all types of becoming.

The view of aesthetics which Nietzsche wants to criticize is one where there is an attempt to detach the artist from the work. This is analogous to what we found in the previous chapter: certain types of morality attempted to dissociate the doer from the deed.[10] Nietzsche was suspicious of ascetic tendencies in ethics; they seem even more absurd and obviously wrong in the case of art. These tendencies were present in morality. He unmasks the interest behind "selfless" morality in the following passage, where he says, "the feelings of devotion, self-sacrifice for one's neighbor, the whole morality of self-denial must be questioned mercilessly and taken to court."[11] Philosophers tend to write about art in a way that claims to be disinterested. The power is taken away by making it "moral," by taming it. The result is that any aesthetic value must meet some moral criterion. We saw this demand present in Nietzsche's understanding of both Plato's and Aristotle's views of art. In this passage from *Beyond Good and Evil*, §33, Nietzsche is beginning to take on Kant's aesthetic views. Kant believes that disinterest on the part of the spectator is a positive value. Nietzsche also mentions this in *On the Genealogy of Morals.* Nietzsche criticizes this view when he speaks of "the aesthetics of 'contemplation devoid of all interest' which is used today as a seductive guise for the emasculation of art, to give it a good conscience."[12] Our fear of the power of art, just as our fear of the power of desire, motivates this peculiar attitude toward it. Nietzsche finds this attitude prevalent in a great deal of philosophical literature.

Nietzsche wants us to always consider both perspectives. He wants to remind us that they are all only perspectives, and that the perspectives produce different views and may even suggest different values.

> Those who create and those who enjoy.—Everyone who enjoys believes the tree was concerned with the fruit; but it was, in fact, concerned about the seed.—It is in this that there lies the difference between those who create and all who enjoy.[13]

In the above quotation from *Assorted Opinions and Maxims* (the second section of *Human, All Too Human*), we can see an instance of the consequences of a shift in perspective. The two groups of people in the metaphor represent differing perspectives on the same situation: those who look at a thing for the purpose of enjoying it, that is, with their own agenda, and those who look at it from the perspective of the purpose of its creation, from the perspective of its creator.

Nietzsche begins the passage by letting us know that he is interested in distinguishing between the creators and the spectators (those who enjoy). These two groups of people represent, in the metaphor, differing perspectives on the same reality. One of the radical consequences of having differing perspectives is actually seeing different entities, or at least giving priority to them. People pick out different features of the same story as relevant to their analysis (the fruit and the seed). Both of the perspectives are involved, but the nature of the involvement is significantly different. In each case there is a different interest which motivates it. The people who enjoy and get pleasure from the product see the purpose behind its creation in the fruit, in that which gives them pleasure. But Nietzsche says, the purpose in the tree's creation is the seed, that which allows it to go on. The fruit in this latter case is only a means to that end, that is, it nourishes the seed.

These are the respective and different "realities" pictured in the example. They show that an entirely different picture of the situation is produced by heterogeneous motivations. Nietzsche says that the purpose of this little example is to show something different about those who create and those who enjoy. He also shows how the difference of interest or perspective will give us different and competing versions of reality.

To extend the metaphor of the tree, let us assume that it is an apple tree, and flesh out his example. In both cases, it is clear to everyone that the tree produces apples (just as the artist produces works). But, Nietzsche is asking, how are we to understand the purpose of the tree? He answers by saying that we look at the fruit, in this case the apple, differently, depending on what our intentions are. The apple is a fruit made for the enjoyment of the person who will eat it, or it is a casing for a seed in order to nourish the seed. In both cases, what is under consideration is the apple, but it is looked at differently, depending upon our intentions toward it. If we make an analogy between the fecundity of the tree, and the fecundity of the artist (another creator), we see that the view of the tree represents a different perspective from that of the enjoyer, critic, or judge. The difference in depiction is so important that, in the case of the tree metaphor, a different entity (seed or fruit) is under consideration, depending upon the perspective from which we choose to look at the situation. The relation between the two entities—seed and fruit—must be seen differently. Nietzsche also suggests that it is the perspective of the tree ("the tree was, in fact, concerned about the seed") which is to be preferred.

The spectator will tend to try to look for enjoyment; the artist will look for the product which gives birth to other creations. Earlier, we looked at *Beyond Good and Evil*, §33. In this section, Nietzsche talks of his suspicions about self-denial in a moral and aesthetic context. He thinks there might be some seduction behind this supposed asceticism and hence he recommends that it be treated with suspicion. He says,

> That they [these values of denial] please—those who have them and those who enjoy their fruits, and also the mere spectator—this does not yet constitute all argument in their favor but rather invites caution. So let us be cautious.

Again, he is continuing to emphasize the fact that not only is this self-denial pleasurable, hence, not terribly self-denying, but also, and more essentially, that a certain perspective is being endorsed in these cases: that of the spectator or "enjoyer." In another passage, Nietzsche explores the relation between the artist and spectator further. In this case we have a spectator of a particular sort: a critic.

> This is what distinguishes the artist from laymen (those susceptible to art): the latter reach the high point of their susceptibility when they receive the former as they give—so that an antagonism between these two gifts is not only natural but desirable. The perspectives of these two states are opposite: to demand of the artist that he should practice the perspective of the audience (of the critic-) means to demand that he should impoverish himself and his creative power.[14]

By making the distinction between creation and appreciation, it is possible to consider a variety of approaches to the study of art. Nietzsche goes on to say that, "It is to the honor of the artist if he is unable to be a critic ...." The fact that some artists are incapable of adopting a spectator's point of view is a mark in their favor. If they are preoccupied with judgment, with "looking back," then they are not completely artists.

Nietzsche believes that most philosophers have displayed their weaknesses and biases when talking about art. The inadequacy of philosophical writings on art can be traced to an anti-sensual, and hence anti-aesthetic, bias in philosophy. A strong disposition toward asceticism and against sensuality is found in philosophy. If philosophers were to reverse these values, it would be enough to have their work considered spurious or suspect. This has been true in Nietzsche's own case. He has been called a poet instead of a philosopher. "Wherever there have been philosophers, ... there has prevailed a special philosopher's resentment against sensuality; ... There likewise exists a properly philosophical prejudice in favor of the ascetic ideal."[15] Nietzsche also sees a value in asceticism which he says provides philosophers with the conditions most favorable to the exercise of their intelligence. But, Nietzsche means the harnessing of the power of the sensual, not its denial and repudiation. The view of most philosophers is that sensuality would "naturally" lead them away from reason or threaten their work.

This Puritanism in philosophy has led to a peculiar attitude toward art (held by philosophers). We saw some examples of this earlier in the case of Plato and Aristotle. Art is not looked at from the perspective of the participant in creation: but, rather, from that of the spectator and judge. As a consequence of this perspective many philosophers, for example, Kant and Arthur Schopenhauer, concentrate on the effects of art on the viewer rather than on the activity of the artist.

> Kant, like all philosophers, instead of viewing the esthetic issue from the side of the artist, envisaged art and beauty solely from the "spectator's" point of view, and so, without himself realizing it, smuggled the "spectator" into the concept of beauty.[16]

The spectator's view is an outsider's point of view. Note that Nietzsche is not just picking out individuals. This is a general comment on a certain type of aesthetic theory. But it is also that of a particular spectator. Nietzsche goes on to say that in Kant's case this is unusually problematic. Kant was neither subtle nor perceptive as an aesthetic spectator.

Because of this turn which, as we have seen, is common to much Western thought, the effect of the artwork on the spectator is considered to be central in most philosophical theories. In viewing and evaluating art, philosophers have attempted to take the work out of the context of its creation. They have also tried to understand art and "elevate" it by seeing it in terms of something else. Art is often given a psychological or moral justification. Schopenhauer, for example, gives an analysis of art which suggests its highest value is as therapy; a release from the will. He says "it counteracts the sexual 'interest'"[17] Not only is it justified as therapy, it is also considered acceptable only when it serves the "higher" ends of morality or politics, as we saw in the cases of Plato and, in his peculiar way, Tolstoy as well. This justification applies, as long as it is in a position of subservience.

Kant, also, tried to give a non-aesthetic (in the sense of non-sensual) justification when he gave prominence to those "predicates of beauty" which flatter the intellect, that is, "impersonality and universality."[18] He believed he was honoring art and beauty when he made them capable of those qualities which attend upon science and philosophy, two unquestionably legitimate enterprises in Kant's mind. In all of these examples, the explanation and justification of aesthetic activity is in terms of other kinds of "legitimate" activity. This serves to divorce it from the sensual realm; and this is supposed to be what elevates it.

We can take Kant as typical of other aesthetic philosophers in his attempt to appeal outside of art for a justification of aesthetic judgment, but he is not typical in giving an "intellectual" interpretation of aesthetic values or concepts. Nietzsche criticizes Kant for his bloodless definition of beauty as that which gives us "disinterested pleasure." But what is wrong with this disinterested, this uninvolved spectator's point of view? It distorts while claiming not to distort. We have seen this above when Kant "smuggled" his own values into the idea of beauty.[19]

In the case of art, we commonly take the spectator's point of view because we have not learned to think of ourselves as artists or creators. This is true even though every day we make hundreds of aesthetic and sensual choices which help to define our taste and create our aesthetic environment. Choice of what we eat, and where, is one example of this. This may seem like an extended sense of the aesthetic. It is, but Nietzsche takes this view on ethics, as we have seen in the second chapter. In the first chapter, Nietzsche talked about "Little Deviant Acts." There he showed how momentous he thought everything we do is. These actions should not seem insignificant. It is all the little things we do in our life that show what we value.[20] In that passage, Nietzsche pointed out the histories which he wanted us to do. They included histories of envy, love, the moral effects of food, and the manners of artists and artisans. All of these are moral or aesthetic activities or values which have not always been considered of great import, certainly not enough so to devote to historical study. These things are terribly important to Nietzsche because, as we act, we create and affirm values. We need to see this in all the aspects of our lives, not just in the major decisions or those which the previous cultures have picked out as especially relevant.

We have seen that Nietzsche wants to criticize our adoption of a disinterested point of view in a variety of contexts. He is skeptical about the possibility of there being such a perspective. Consequently, he approaches with suspicion any attempt to move toward a view which claims to achieve or approximate a disinterested (or perspectiveless) view. In views which claim to be disinterested, Nietzsche enjoys unmasking the supposed "lack of interest" and showing the motivation which lay behind the presumed neutrality of philosophic inquiry. For example, he considers, "How malicious philosophers can be!" In the work of Epicurus, he finds a criticism of Plato which leads him to speculate: "he [Epicurus], that old schoolmaster from Samos, who sat, hidden away, in his little garden at Athens and wrote three hundred books—who knows [why]? perhaps from rage and ambition against Plato?"[21] In his evaluations of theories Nietzsche always evaluates the person with the work.[22] In *Philosophy in the Tragic Age of the Greeks* Nietzsche says, "The only thing of interest in a refuted system is the personal element."[23] Even in the case where a perspective is admitted by an author, we have seen him call into question a particular perspective, that is, that of the judge, spectator, or "enjoyer." The perspective of the outsider is suspect because it seems to fill an atavistic need, one tied to days when we believed a disinterested view was possible.

The perspective of acknowledged involvement is to be preferred as one which is "the least false." Nietzsche is interested in either the critic with the admitted motivation, for example, enjoyment, or the obviously involved perspective of the participant in creation: the artist. The issue of perspective bears weight in all aspects of our life. The perspective of a living, experiencing person (which is necessarily responsive to change and flux) is the one Nietzsche wants to explore more carefully. To extend this to the moral sphere: we are not merely spectators in morality; we are participants in life.

In another example of unmasking interest, again in the case of Kant, Nietzsche speaks of the personal arrogance of the man, of his pride in answering the question: how are synthetic a priori judgments possible? The answer? "'by virtue of a faculty'—he [Kant] had said or, at least, meant. But is this an answer? An explanation? Or is it rather merely a repetition of the question?"[24] Nietzsche compares this to Moliere's nonsense explanation by a doctor in one of his plays. The doctor "explains" how opium induces sleep: "Because it contains a sleepy faculty whose nature it is to put the senses to sleep." The "faculty" hunting started by Kant and continued by his successors accepts such unsatisfactory answers. This sleepy faculty which has not awakened to the absurdity of this type of explanation has put the senses to sleep. Put them to sleep because it gave them ammunition to counteract the "predominant sensualism which overflowed from the last century."

In the above passage, Nietzsche again ties together his suspicions about pure, disinterested inquiry with an anti-sensuous bias on the part of the inquirers.[25] He talks in the same passage about the "finding" of these faculties: "The honeymoon of German philosophy arrived. All the young theologians of the Tübingen seminary went into the bushes looking for 'faculties.' And what they did not find ... when one cannot yet distinguish between 'finding' and 'inventing'!" To counteract this philosophical mythology, Nietzsche recommends that we again substitute a psychological question for a metaphysical or epistemological one. We should do this when considering Kant's question: "how are synthetic a priori judgments possible?" We should translate this into "Why is belief in such judgments necessary?"[26]

The perspective of the spectator is relevant to evaluation, according to Nietzsche; but, according to Kant, an interested pleasure would be a corrupt pleasure. It would be biased by trivial, personal and social concerns; it would lack universality. The sensual, the individual, in short, the phenomenal have moved us away from reason and the purely intellectual realms which are properly those of the philosopher. But Nietzsche is claiming that it is Kant who is doing the distorting. Kant has that common philosophical bias or skepticism about the phenomenal world (he was never quite able to let go of the noumenal world although he kept it beyond our reach), the world of which we are a part. His pessimism about the value of this world and about the possibility of obtaining the kind of truth he would like, reliable, repeatable, certain, make him take the bizarre perspective upon art which he does.

Nietzsche asks would it not be more sensible to consider the artist in the historical and cultural context with the art work. This would be relevant both in order to understand it and to evaluate it. Perhaps this "unphilosophical" (when viewed as a methodology) point of view is left over from Nietzsche's philological training. Nietzsche considers the cultural context relevant to the evaluation of art, and the art as relevant to the evaluation of a culture. We judge a culture by the art it produces. We will examine this when we look at his *The Birth of Tragedy*.

So far, in Nietzsche's critique of philosophical writings on art, there is a move similar to the turn away from metaphysics. We found that turn imaged by the death of God. In this case, we again find a philosopher trying to make an assessment from outside merely by applying categories to the single instance: the artwork or beautiful object. The philosopher is trying to attain or adopt a perspective which transcends the life of the participants in aesthetic culture. Not only the philosopher, but the religious thinker and moralist, all try to judge from outside of the experience. Their thought is respectively "other-worldly" in the sense of transcendence through reason, "other-worldly" in the sense of belief in another real world, or "other-worldly" by being external to the situation. This idea is validated by an appeal to a cultural community which is already in place, and therefore legitimized. Thus an empiricist ethic, like utilitarianism, does not escape this criticism.

These aesthetic philosophers judge from the outside, and they then set up as standards values which have a justification in realms where they are comfortable, namely, outside of art. So, again under the pretense of avoiding distortion, we find we have quite specific distortions which arise from these peculiar and particular perspectives. In this case it is not just a perspective which is outside the world, but rather one which comes from some fixed system of values whether that originates in a metaphysical or a moral system, and whether that system is justified by a transcendental appeal or by an appeal to a community of shared laws.

What Nietzsche is trying to do is to involve us in the world where we live and, in this case, to look at the worldly origin of art and aesthetic value. Again we are asked to come down to earth, to consider the earthly (as opposed to the divine or spiritual discussed above in relation to inspiration) origin of ideas and ideals of beauty and art, to consider the cultural and individual origin of the art work in our society and history. Nietzsche has extended his critique into the aesthetic realm. Here we have seen that philosophy tries to look at art once again from a removed perspective: the perspective of a critic or judge. Such philosophers believe that judgments should be disinterested; Kant gives us our most extreme example of this model. We have already seen that, except for the case of an empty hypothetical (for example, God), Nietzsche believes that there is no disinterested perspective (might we not even conclude that God's perspective was interested?)

We will see an example of a "good" critic in Chapter Four. In that case we will have an involved judgment, one which puts the critic at risk—going beyond the safe criteria of a theory of artistic value. The interest and concern of the inquirer is not a liability; it is, rather, that which makes inquiry possible:

> ... the great passion of the seeker after knowledge who lives and must live continually in the thundercloud of the highest problems and the heaviest responsibilities (by no means as an observer, outside, indifferent, secure, and objective).[27]

Without interest there would be no questions to begin inquiry. Since we cannot avoid perspectival knowing, we might rather acknowledge it. This is precisely what Nietzsche does, and also what other philosophers attack him for—his ungentlemanly, immodest revelation of his ends, his presuppositions and his methods, especially as he unmasks and uncovers theirs.

Nietzsche wants to know what would be the value of having the "bad" type of judge, the one we find recommended by the philosophers. The judge will be conservative, judging by the standards of the past, of what we collectively think. This is what we as a culture have projected upon the heavens, but what in reality represents our values, that which binds us together as a culture. But a culture is not, according to Nietzsche, a static thing; and the belief that it is, that there exist absolute or transcendental values, is worrisome. This piece of dogma (and dogmatism in general) is ridiculed by Nietzsche in the preface to *Beyond Good and Evil*, as the "most dangerous of all errors so far ... Plato's invention of the pure spirit and the good as such."[28] The good as such, the good in itself, are the Platonic and Kantian inventions which deny the perspectival, the relational character of knowing and evaluation. The idea of pure spirit precipitated the divorce between the sensual and the spiritual which eventually takes the form of reason versus lust in Christianity. This was discussed in Chapter One. It is worth looking at the matter again.[29]

> The Christian priest is from the first a mortal enemy of sensuality: no greater antithesis can be imagined than the innocently awed and solemn attitude adopted by, e.g., the most honorable women's cults in Athens in the presence of the symbols of sex. The act of procreation is the mystery as such in all nonascetic religions: a sort of symbol of perfection and of the mysterious design of the future: rebirth, immortality.[30]

Nietzsche is interested in countering this anti-sensual and anti-sexual bias. He uses sexual metaphors and reverses the values of Christianity that suggests that the sexual, and particularly the sensual, bring us down. He says instead that: "The degree and kind of a man's sexuality reach up into the ultimate pinnacle of his spirit."[31] In Nietzsche's criticism of Parmenides which he published earlier in *Philosophy in the Tragic Age of the Greeks*, he had spoken of "the falsehood inherent in the absolute separation of senses and concepts, and in the identity of being and thinking ...."[32] Speaking of Parmenides, he says:

> By wrenching apart the senses and the capacity for abstraction, in other words by splitting up mind as though it were composed of two quite separate capacities, he demolished intellect itself, encouraging man to indulge in that wholly erroneous distinction between "spirit" and "body" which, especially since Plato, lies upon philosophy like a curse. All sense perceptions, says Parmenides, yield but illusions .... All the manifold colorful world known to experience, all the transformations of its qualities, all the orderliness of its ups and downs, are cast aside mercilessly as mere semblance and illusion. Nothing may be learned from them.[33]

This regrettable occurrence dictated that "Henceforward truth shall live only in the palest, most abstracted generalities, in the empty husks of the most indefinite terms, ..."[34] In *Beyond Good and Evil*, Nietzsche talks about how in the setting up of these dichotomies and oppositions they are transformed from aspects or properties of things into substances, and hence we have the birth of a pernicious metaphysics. The identification of being and thinking which continues in the work of Plato and Descartes also gives us a "falsification" which helps to bring about or reinforces the divorce between mind or soul and body.

One of Nietzsche's purposes in choosing to look at philosophers' treatment of art is that it is a point of the Western philosopher's weakness. This is true for the reasons we have just been discussing. It usually includes their treatment of the sensual. In this treatment it is possible to see whether or not they are simply conforming to the Platonic, Christian, Puritanical denigration of the world of change. If they merely accept the above mentioned dichotomy, Nietzsche is going to be suspicious of their depth. He will suspect that, in spite of their rhetoric and innovations, they are, like Kant, at bottom only "deeply" conventional (in the convention that, from Plato to Christianity, accepted this divorce between reason and desire). One of the dilemmas in which this puts Nietzsche is that, since most of Western philosophy conforms to this description, it must be dismissed. It is puzzling that Nietzsche does not find Aristotle more congenial in this respect. It is easy enough to see why Aristotle's essentialism or virtue ethic, what Nietzsche calls "the harmless mean," would be unattractive to him. After all, Aristotle is a Puritan morally but not metaphysically. Most of Nietzsche's mention of Aristotle concentrates on the *Poetics*, and Aristotle is not seen as a kindred spirit.

Heraclitus is an exception to the dismissal of so much Western philosophy, again from Nietzsche's early work:

> Heraclitus's regal possession is his extraordinary power to think intuitively. Toward the other type of thinking, the type that is accomplished in concepts and logical combinations, in other words toward reason, he shows himself cool, insensitive, in fact hostile, and seems to feel pleasure whenever he can contradict it with an intuitively arrived at truth. He does this in dicta like "Everything forever has its opposite along with it," and in such unabashed fashion that Aristotle accused him of the highest crime before the tribunal of reason: to have sinned against the law of contradiction. But intuitive thinking embraces two things: one, the present many colored and changing world that crowds in upon us in all our experiences, and, two, the conditions which alone make any experience of this world possible: time and space.[35]

Nietzsche must go outside Christian culture and its antecedents in Platonism. He does this, as we have seen, by looking at pre-Socratic antiquity and by looking at artists who, in an anti-aesthetic culture, must be rebels (he also looks at sexuality and love).

Nietzsche, in effect, wants an aesthetic revolution as well as a philosophical one. It might be more correct to say that the philosophical (methodological), aesthetic, and moral are part of the same revolution. Nietzsche believes that contemporary art is stifled by the anti-sensual elements of our cultural heritage. This is part of the reason Wagner, with his resurrection of the medieval Teutonic myths, looms so large in Nietzsche's early, hopeful writings. Wagner is the new counter-Christian. Nietzsche's eventual rejection of Wagner is based on what Nietzsche perceives as his turning back to Christian life-denying values. The nationalism and anti-Semitism which Nietzsche saw Wagner eventually coming to serve were base because they were political. They serve the state, they represent putting these types of concerns above aesthetic ones, so that once again art is in service to morality. Again we have a view of art which is deeply conventional (in this sense serving the Platonic or Christian metaphysics)—a profoundly disappointing turn of events for Nietzsche. It is wrong to be conventional when the conventions are harmful, or no longer useful, and do not conduce to our self-overcoming.

We are not just judges with respect to art any more than we are with respect to morality. We are actors and participants in our culture (regardless of the ambiguity of our relations with it if we are also innovators). Nietzsche is often looked at as being the advocate of the *Übermensch*, the Siegfried, the lonely hero who stands against culture. But this is quite mistaken. Nietzsche understands that the position of both the reformer and the rebel is within culture and that culture is not a static thing, nor are the values one should have above or beyond a given culture. They are in it and of it while they project a reality outside of it.

He says:

> Only aesthetic man can look thus at the world, a man who has experienced in artists and in the birth of art objects how the struggle of the many can yet carry rules and laws inherent in itself, how the artist stands contemplatively above and at the same time actively within his work, how necessity and random play, oppositional tension and harmony must pair to create a work of art.[36]

Nietzsche understands quite well the ambiguous position of the rebel or innovator whether moral or aesthetic—perhaps because he himself is one—to be both inside and outside of a culture. The artist wants the attention of the people, their love and their interest, at the same time realizing that it will not be given as long as he or she fails to conform. He writes in "The Philosopher as Cultural Physician":

> If they are abnormal, then surely they have nothing to do with the people? This is not the case: the people need the anomalies even if the anomalies do not exist for the people's sake.[37]

The work of art provides evidence for this: the creator himself understands the work; nevertheless, it has a side which is turned toward the public.

Nietzsche realizes these difficulties in his own case, as well as that of other creative artists and "revolutionaries." As a revolutionary one's effects may be minimal; one may be a "posthumous thinker" (unrewarded in one's life), speaking to those "as yet unborn." This is not just Nietzsche's personal arrogance speaking (although certainly it is partially so), it is also a part of what he believes to be the reality of the situation. Nietzsche realizes that even those who support the artists often only half understand them (certainly in his own case, until Georg Brandes, he is not even half understood), or worse, misunderstand them. Nietzsche feared that he might only have followers, not inspire new innovators. Hence my evaluation of Foucault, whom I think Nietzsche would have been proud to have as a successor.

The ambiguities of the situation of an artist are expressed wonderfully in *Zarathustra*, in the main character's continual descents and retreats, his goings both over and under the people but never quite with them. It is full of the intense disappointments and the joys of self-overcoming which are peculiar to the artist or innovator.

The artists stand, to a certain extent, outside of culture and yet also within it. They must create works which go beyond it. But, to Nietzsche, the aesthetic products are cultural; they are not produced merely by the lonely, rebellious artist. This is at odds with a great deal of Nietzsche scholarship, especially post-World War I, but it is born out if one considers his work as a whole. The early philological writings and notes concentrate on the cultural context and significance of creation whether it be aesthetic or philosophical. *The Birth of Tragedy* continues to look at opposing or different cultural values in the course of the history of a growing or declining culture. This is true both in its treatment of Greek antiquity and of contemporary German culture. Nietzsche's more mature work, his most sophisticated history, *On the Genealogy of Morals* does the same thing.

The aesthetic example which Nietzsche explores on a cultural scale is the changing of cultural and aesthetic values found in early Greek culture. In his history of *The Birth of Tragedy from the Spirit of Music*, Nietzsche studies a history of artistic development and of the changing values which artists espouse. In the earlier part of this essay he considers the art forms which allowed Greek tragic artists to make tragedy. Greek tragedy was a synthesis of a number of these cultural and artistic elements. Nietzsche gives an unusual interpretation of the elements which contribute to the unique form of tragedy which we find in the work of Sophocles and Aeschylus. In contrast, Euripides, usually seen with Socrates as part of the Golden Age of Athens, is seen as a decadent. The more common interpretations of Greek cultural history find the later Hellenistic works decadent. In the visual arts this art stresses the representation of emotion, ethnic diversity, and people of different ages as against the depiction of the young men and women represented in the so called "Classical" period. The latter part of Nietzsche's essay looks for such a synthesis or at least the countering of Christian "pessimism" (or other-worldliness) in the art of contemporary Germany and most specifically in Wagnerian opera.

At this point we will briefly go over some of his discussion of this "birth." We will not be particularly concerned here with the larger aim of the essay with regard to Wagner and contemporary German culture. Our purpose will be twofold. On the one hand we will try to see the values in early antiquity which Nietzsche is interested in reclaiming. Special attention will be paid to the values he later associates with the god Dionysus. This god is not identical to the god we find in the early works, but is a synthesis of a variety of ideas and values many of which Nietzsche found in antiquity. On the other hand, our purpose is to look at Nietzsche's method. In *The Birth of Tragedy*, Nietzsche gives us his first published "genealogy."[38] We will compare this genesis with that of values in the Western, especially Christian tradition which we have explored in the last two sections. In both cases, what Nietzsche does is create and find a history for that which is supposedly without a history. The high point, the classical age of Greek art is supposed to stand out from other ages as one apart, embodying the perfection of certain ideals. This is supposed to be true because of the superiority of the artistic products. Winckelmann's views, which we will consider further on, and other more romantic treatments, are examples of a type of approach that begins with the assumption of superiority based upon "objective" aesthetic values. Nietzsche forces us to look at Greek art in its context and history. He then revises the assessment of art in that period.

In *The Birth of Tragedy*, Nietzsche sets out to explore the genesis of tragic drama. He traces its inception to the dithyrambic choruses of the early Greeks. (Although none of these early works survive, there are later examples of the dithyramb, for example, in Pindar). The dithyramb is thought to be a choric song blended with some kind of movement or dance which is vehement or wild in character. The whole ritual is done in honor of the god Dionysus. After this beginning, the dithyramb developed into the chorus of Attic tragedy. Nietzsche traces the significance of that chorus through the work of the major tragedians: Aeschylus, Sophocles and, in its waning significance, in Euripides.

As the subtitle to the first edition implies, Nietzsche sees the "birth" of tragedy as coming out of or from the spirit of music. He juxtaposes two ideas which, by their "constant conflicts and periodic acts of reconciliation,"[39] give birth to this higher art form: Greek tragedy. Nietzsche, as he often does, here uses the example of sexual strife, love, and procreation to give us an image of this blending. He then uses the gods Dionysus and Apollo as images or symbols of these two tendencies, which become major elements in Greek culture. These contrasting and (when they come together in Attic tragedy) complementary ideas are characterized as combining most of the main dualities present in Greek thought. They are cultural tendencies projected into the aesthetic output of the people. Apollo and Dionysus represent, for example, respectively; limit and the unlimited, singularity and multiplicity, individual and collective, form and matter, self-determination and loss of self, moderation and excess. These opposing dualities exhibit themselves in human life "physiologically" as dream and intoxication, in the drama as the hero and the chorus, in art (in general) as sculpture and dance.

The Dionysian is taken to be a primal impulse. The worship of Dionysus is a much more ancient practice, and this makes it more likely that it actually had the historical ties to the dithyramb which Nietzsche suggests. He mentions in his notes how this element of Greek culture has not been given due notice because "An adverse fate decreed that the late and decadent forms of Hellenism should exert the greatest historical interest ... [but] One must know the younger Greece in great detail in order to differentiate it from the older."[40]

The Dionysian wisdom is revealed in the wisdom of Silenus, which tells us that the most desirable thing for human beings is "not to be born, not to *be*, to be *nothing*. But the second best for you is—to die soon."[41] This is taken by Nietzsche as the folk wisdom of the more ancient Greeks. He speaks of the Olympian host (Apollinian) as created to counteract this more ancient wisdom.

> Apollo is at once the god of all plastic powers and the soothsaying god. He who is etymologically the "lucent" one, the god of light, reigns also over the fair illusion of our inner world of fantasy. The perfection of these conditions in contrast to our imperfectly understood waking reality, as well as our profound awareness of nature's healing powers during the interval of sleep and dream, furnishes a symbolic analogue to the soothsaying faculty and quite generally to the arts, which make life possible and worth living. But the image of Apollo must incorporate that thin line which the dream image may not cross, under penalty of becoming pathological, of

> imposing itself on us as crass reality: a discreet limitation, a freedom from all extravagant urges, the sapient tranquility of the plastic god. His eyes must be sunlike, in keeping with his origin. Even at those moments when he is angry and ill-tempered there lies upon him the consecration of fair illusion.[42]

The god Apollo is essentially a god of limit and delineation. This god is appropriate to the plastic arts, just as the lack of limitation is appropriate to music and the Dionysian.

Nietzsche wants to emphasize the mutual dependency of these gods who are also archetypes. Apollo, despite:

> ... all [his] beauty and moderation, his entire existence rested on a hidden substratum, of suffering and of knowledge, revealed to him by the Dionysian. And behold: Apollo could not live without Dionysus! The "titanic" and the "barbaric" were in the last analysis as necessary as the Apollinian.[43]

The god of prudent rationalism was dependent upon the god of intoxication and excess. Both of these elements are brought together in the art of Aeschylus (524-455 BC) and Sophocles (495-405 BC), where their union forms the apotheosis of the tragic art. Nietzsche says:

> This view of things already provides us with all the elements of a profound and pessimistic view of the world, together with the *mystery doctrine of tragedy*: the fundamental knowledge of the oneness of everything existent, the conception of individuation as the primal cause of evil, and of art as the joyous hope that the spell of individuation may be broken in augury of a restored oneness.[44]

But this high art is destroyed, in Nietzsche's view, by Euripides (c. 483-406 BC) and also Socrates (c. 470-399 BC), who is said to have influenced him. Myth and music die under reason. He considers Euripides's art to be a "flight from seriousness and terror."[45] Euripides adopts the Socratic aesthetic; that "to be beautiful everything must be intelligible"—cool thoughts replace Apollinian contemplation; fiery effects replace Dionysian ecstasy.[46] It is a watering down of the high tragic art by "audacious reasonableness."

In the elevated work of Aeschylus, fate was above the gods and human beings, as eternal justice. In the Oedipus cycle of Sophocles, the hypertrophy of reason in a mortal is punished.[47] Only in Euripides is the scale reduced to the mortal, the merely moral; in other words, Dionysus is no longer the hero in disguise of the drama.[48] When we see this, we have reached "... the real goal of our investigation, which is directed toward knowledge of the Dionysian-Apollinian genius and its art product, or at least toward some feeling for and understanding of this mystery of union."[49]

If we take Nietzsche as having achieved his purpose in these earlier sections on antiquity, the question arises: How are we to take this text and in a sense what is its purpose? As a work of philology it is at least unorthodox. If Nietzsche's friend and colleague Erwin Rohde's scholarly book *Psyche* (published in 1893) is a typical example of nineteenth-century scholarly work in the field, we immediately see that Nietzsche's work will not fit in with the pure, "objective," copiously footnoted, text typical of German philology. Rohde, in fact, had to come to Nietzsche's defense in attacks upon Nietzsche's "unprofessionalism."[50]

In order to understand Nietzsche's approach to Hellenism and philology, we need to look at some of his writings on the topic.

> There is a certain kind of thoroughness which is but the excuse for inactivity. Think of what Goethe understood about antiquity: certainly not as much as any philologist, and yet quite enough to enable him to engage in fruitful struggle with it. One *should* not, in fact, know more about a thing than one can oneself digest creatively. Moreover the only means of truly understanding anything is one's attempt to *do* it. Let us try to live in the manner of the ancients—and we shall instantly come a hundred miles closer to them than with all our learnedness. Our philologists nowhere demonstrate that they somehow strive to vie with antiquity; that is why *their* antiquity is without any effect on the schools.[51]

Nietzsche is critical of the sterile scholarship he sees around him in the universities and schools.[52] Yet, *The Birth of Tragedy* must be addressed to those familiar enough with the works involved to make a judgment on its thesis. Nietzsche must have wanted a reader who would evaluate and weigh his insights (as he was later to do in his testing for sound values, tapping them with a tuning hammer to see if they had an authentic ring). This is the kind of history he describes in *Untimely Meditations*, "On the Uses and Disadvantages of History for Life." In the passage below he describes why we need history.

> We need history, certainly, but we need it for reasons different from those for which the idler in the garden of knowledge needs it, even though he may look nobly down on our rough and charmless needs and requirements. We need it, that is to say, for the sake of life and action, not so as to turn comfortably away from life and action, let alone for the purpose of extenuating the self-seeking life and the base and cowardly action. We want to serve history only to the extent that history serves life: for it is possible to value the study of history to such a degree that life becomes stunted and degenerate—a phenomenon we are now forced to acknowledge, painful though this may be, in the face of certain striking

symptoms of our age.[53]

History must help us to live; it must have an application in our lives. The study of other cultures must make a difference to us. The values of another culture will matter to us only if we live them and try them on. History must become genealogy. It must be motivated by issues arising in our life and it must matter to us.

Walter Kaufmann calls *The Birth of Tragedy* "one of the most suggestive and influential studies of tragedy ever written."[54] Let us overlook the stylistic considerations, the "youthful vigor" and other criticisms of the book which have been dealt with by Kaufmann and very perceptively by Nietzsche himself.[55] The book is putting forth a novel and controversial thesis and, since tradition is necessary for revolution, we should explore the background in which this work was set. Historically, the greater part of the emphasis on Greek civilization has been on the higher "stages" of Greek art, the so-called classical age of the fifth century. Nietzsche's close attention to the earlier phases is, as he himself points out, unusual. But the real turnabout lies in his viewing Euripides and Socrates as decadents, which amounts to philological sacrilege.[56] These figures are usually considered to be at the height of classical antiquity, not representative of its decline.

But Nietzsche is not without his own romantic conception of the Hellenes. As already mentioned, he does not seek to maintain the "objectivity" which reached its height in nineteenth-century German scholarship. He is, even at this relatively early date, suspicious of any "disinterestedness." Yet, Nietzsche is also attacking some of the romantic notions of the eighteenth-century, more specifically the "pseudo idealism" of Goethe and Johann Friedrich von Schiller. Goethe and Schiller's notions of Greece were largely based upon the work of, and their acquaintance with, Johann Joachim Winckelmann (1711-1768), the archeologist and art historian. Winckelmann's view of the Greeks is typified by his famous phrase "*edle Einfach und stille Gro(e)sse*," noble simplicity and quiet/tranquil grandeur. Winckelmann, Goethe, Schiller, and for that matter Nietzsche himself, never went to Greece, although all but Schiller were for a time in Italy.[57]

In the visual arts, this characterization of restraint and nobility was based upon Winckelmann's experience of Roman copies of works about which he could only conjecture. Under his influence, Goethe writes that "antiquity belongs to nature and where antiquity speaks to us it is the most natural nature," where security, perfection, and instinctive reason blend. In Schiller we find the self-conscious man looking back on an unconscious age, seeking nature as a consolation for life and reality. Against these views, Nietzsche writes:

> Winckelmann's and Goethe's Greeks, Victor Hugo's orientals, Wagner's Edda characters, Walter Scott's Englishmen of the thirteenth century—some day the whole comedy will be exposed! it was all historically false beyond measure, *but*—modern.[58]

We have found in these works what we wanted to find, something which justified a "modern" taste.

For the romantic view mentioned above, Nietzsche substitutes a more complicated and by this time better documented view of Greek culture. Not that he bothers to give us documentation in this text. He introduces and emphasizes the terrible, the suffering, the morally repulsive, symbolized in a god who is dismembered by his followers in a ritual frenzy.

But in Nietzsche's approach to this conception of the Greeks, how different is he from the eighteenth-century Greco-philes? As a young man he wrote, "The Greeks have surely never been overvalued."[59] I think that part of Nietzsche's infatuation comes from the fact that in Greek culture we find the only alternative to Christian culture which is really fleshed out. We have seen his occasional reference to oriental culture, which also intrigued him, but he was not sufficiently aware of the particularities of those cultures to deal with them in more than a cursory manner.

With this background, let us now return to Nietzsche's views on art and life: In *The Birth of Tragedy* Nietzsche had said, "... it is only as an *aesthetic phenomenon* that existence and the world are eternally *justified*."[60] Kaufmann takes this quotation as the thesis of *Nietzsche: Philosopher, Psychologist, Antichrist*.[61] He suggests that Nietzsche himself recognizes only aesthetic values. This quotation refers rather to his characterization of a certain view of art, a Dionysian one. This is set against the aesthetic philosophy of Schopenhauer. Nietzsche has been taking issue with Schopenhauer's view of music. Specifically, he is criticizing the distinction between the subjective and objective which Schopenhauer uses to evaluate the arts. Schopenhauer's "salvation" (see above: the release from the will) is largely aesthetic, but it is also ascetic. Nietzsche wants to overcome Schopenhauer's self-negation with an affirmation.[62] Nietzsche writes:

> The metaphysical comfort—with which, I am suggesting even now, every true tragedy leaves us—that life is at the bottom of things, despite all the changes of appearances, indestructibly powerful and pleasurable—this comfort appears in incarnate clarity in the chorus of satyrs .... With this chorus the profound Hellene, uniquely susceptible to the tenderest and deepest suffering, comforts himself .... Art saves him, and through art life.[63]

Here we find the other possibility which Nietzsche holds up against the pessimism of "the wisest men of all ages have judged alike: *it is no good*."[64] The idea of saving the world through art is not new. We find it in Schiller's *Letters on the Aesthetic Education of Man* and in the second part of Goethe's *Faust*, but Nietzsche will transform those ideas.

In the middle of *The Birth of Tragedy*, Nietzsche talks about the Dionysian reality. He suggests that at one stage, or under some condition, the Dionysian gives us a true perception of the world—where we cast aside the "veil of Maya" and see things as they are. "The muses of the arts of 'illusion' paled before an art that in its intoxication spoke the truth"; "Excess revealed itself as truth." In an early note Nietzsche writes, "Socrates, let me confess it, is so close to me that I am almost constantly doing battle with him."[65] Nietzsche turns Plato on his head. Plato is merely the systematizer of Socrates and it is with Socrates himself that Nietzsche has his most impassioned quarrel. As we have already seen, Socrates is the corrupter of art: this is far worse to Nietzsche than the corruption of the youth.[66]

The decline of Greek culture comes about with the introduction of reason, rather, a certain conception of reason. This is one which ignores reason's dependence upon other elements of life. So long as the element of reason was represented by Apollo, it was dependent upon the Dionysian, upon the wisdom of Silenus, which it endeavored to disguise or temper. But once reason is taken for itself or in itself—once that delicate balance is upset—we have decadence. Without the balance of the willful Dionysian and the limiting Apollo, ascendancy and even action become impossible, and decline will follow.

In Nietzsche's later writings, Dionysus becomes a symbol for a synthesis between this earlier image of the god who can look on all the suffering and misery of life without flinching, and Apollo the god of reason. Then Dionysus comes to symbolize the ability to transcend a number of dichotomies. In Chapter One we have seen this dissolution in the case of the "true" and "apparent" world. This dissolution is something Nietzsche thinks quite desirable. Now, in an aesthetic context, we find:

> That the artist esteems appearance higher than reality is no objection to this proposition [that the distinction between "appearance" and reality is a sign of decadence]. For "appearance" in this case means reality *once more*, only by way of selection, reinforcement, and correction. The tragic artist is no pessimist; he is precisely the one who says Yes to everything questionable, even to the terrible—he is Dionysian ....[67]

One of the dichotomies the god Dionysus helps us transcend is that between the subject and the object. This is mentioned above in Schopenhauer's work. Nietzsche believes that this distinction is "irrelevant to aesthetics."

> Only insofar as the genius in the act of artistic creation coalesces with this primordial artist of the world, does he know anything of the eternal essence of art; for in this state he is, in a marvelous manner, like the weird image of the fairy tale which can turn its eyes at will and behold itself; he is at once subject and object, at once poet, actor and spectator.[68]

In *The Birth of Tragedy* Nietzsche talks about the Dionysian artist who represents a unity; the primordial unity of instinct and desire. Thus, it is not the bloodless unity of a Parmenides, a Plato, and the Christian God.

We should now turn to what Nietzsche has to say in a positive sense, and most of this he gets from Greek antiquity. We have seen that Nietzsche uses the Greeks as another model of how to live in much the same way that one engaged in comparative anthropology might. He wants to look at something that is substantially different from Christianity, and in the West, from Euripides and Socrates on, he cannot find views that are sufficiently different. Classical studies are "untimely," they are different from our time, and it is because of this that they have such a precious value for us.

> ... I do not know what meaning classical studies could have for our time if they were not untimely—that is to say, acting counter to our time and thereby acting on our time and, let us hope, for the benefit of a time to come.[69]

In Greek culture and philosophy, Nietzsche finds an emphasis on the relation of knowledge to the experience of living. He thinks that such a demand should be made on the philosophy and philology of his day. Nietzsche reclaims for philosophy these ideas, with the expectation that they will bring an infusion of refreshing ideas much needed in contemporary European culture, because of its dismal and pessimistic Christian world view.

Along with this reclamation, Nietzsche has also sought an example or a metaphor for our everyday creativity; the creativity which constitutes us as persons. So to the demand for vitality from Antiquity is added the experience of the artist, with its openness and its power to transform.

> *What one should learn from artists*. —How can we make things beautiful, attractive, and desirable for us when they are not? And I rather think that in themselves they never are ... artists [who] are really continually trying to bring off such inventions and feats. Moving away from things until there is a good deal that one no longer sees and there is much that our eye has to add if we are still to see them at all; or seeing things around a corner and as cut out and framed; or to place them so that they partially conceal each other and grant us only glimpses of architectural perspectives; or looking at them through tinted glass or in the light of the sunset; or giving them a surface and skin that is not fully transparent—all this we should learn from artists while being wiser than they are in other matters. For with them this subtle power usually comes to an end where art ends and life begins; but we want to be the poets of our life—first of all in the smallest, most everyday matters.[70]

In the next chapter we will explore this transformation. We will see how it occurs in individuals in the daily events of their lives, and in a culture in the process of its own creation.

Chapter Four

AESTHETICS AND THE NEW PERSPECTIVE OF PHILOSOPHY

> *One must learn to love.*—This is what happens to us in music: First one has to *learn to hear* a figure and melody at all, to detect and distinguish it, to isolate it and delimit it as a separate life. Then it requires some exertion and good will to *tolerate* it in spite of its strangeness, to be patient with its appearance and expression, and kindhearted about its oddity. Finally there comes a moment when we are *used* to it, when we wait for it, when we sense that we should miss it if it were missing; and now it continues to compel and enchant us relentlessly until we have become its humble and enraptured lovers who desire nothing better from the world than it and only it.[1]

Why does Nietzsche turn to art? In the notes collected as *The Will to Power*, Nietzsche writes, "Our religion, morality, and philosophy are decadence forms of man. The *counter-movement: art.*"[2] Nietzsche sees his own time as one of decadence;[3] the declining values for him are, again, not the standard Christian ones of a decline into sensuality. Nietzsche's values represent an affirmation of a healthy sensuality, one which is not in reaction to opposing values, but rather one that asserts itself from a sense of overfullness.

What does Nietzsche mean by the overfullness of these artists? They do not create in order to make up for a deficiency either in the world or in themselves. Instead they create out of their own good feeling about themselves or the world. His point is that they create out of excess or abundance instead of need. They also need not affirm only the tame or unthreatening elements of life. Life in all of its aspects can be incorporated because they do not live in fear of them.

> He that is richest in the fullness of life, the Dionysian god and man, cannot only afford the sight of the terrible and questionable but even the terrible deed and any luxury of destruction, decomposition, and negation. In his case, what is evil, absurd, and ugly seems, as it were, permissible, owing to an excess of procreating, fertilizing energies that can still turn any desert into lush farmland.[4]

It is necessary to distinguish between these types of art. The kind of constraints which motivate an art "dictated by need," poison it. Nietzsche calls these latter artists ones "who suffer from the *impoverishment of life* and seek rest, stillness, calm seas, redemption from themselves through art and knowledge, or intoxication, convulsions, anaesthesia, and madness."[5] It will be noted that in this characterization we see some of the same features which form the motivation for his critique of Christianity.

Nietzsche comes to judge the artist in terms of those values which we more commonly associate with the evaluation of culture. The ways these values are expressed in this context are as follows: "Regarding artists of all kinds, I now avail myself of this main distinction: is it the *hatred* against life or the *excess* of life which has here become creative?"[6]

According to Nietzsche there is no privileged position, no absolute truth, no good in itself but there are different goods, truths, and positions. And these various things can be evaluated. This is not done by taking them out of context or judging them against some ideal, and hence unreal (nonexistent) standard, but by seeing them in context—in relation to the person who created them. Then we can consider what they produce and are. What are the effects of believing in something? How is our life affected? The evaluation always goes back to the person who is actively involved in the creation.

Nietzsche does not look at the phenomenon of creation only in terms of the individual's life. It is looked at in terms of the whole culture of a people who share certain beliefs and practices. Our culture has an extremely long history of belief in *a* truth, in a transcendental source of value. It is necessary for Nietzsche to try to find a model for values and truth which is not insignificant and yet does change in response to historical and cultural ideas and practices. In the history of art or in art itself Nietzsche finds such a model. This is possible in spite of the fact that some philosophers have tried to make of art a repository for their transcendental theories (we have seen instances of this in the previous chapter).

> *The picture of life.*—The task of painting the picture of life, however often poets and philosophers may pose it, is nonetheless senseless: even under the hands of the greatest of painter-thinkers all that has ever eventuated is pictures and miniatures *out of one* life, namely their own—and nothing else is even possible. Something in course of becoming cannot be reflected as a firm and lasting image, as a 'the', in something else in course of becoming.[7]

The "picture of life" is no more real than the "thing-in-itself." Instead, pictures of life are the things which reflect the life of the artist; these are pictures "out of one life." "Life" is only many lives in the course of becoming.

We have seen in the cases of Plato, Aristotle, Tolstoy, and Kant that philosophers have used the fact that aesthetic values change as an argument against them. These values exist in response to issues outside themselves, they are not autonomous. The commissioning of art works and designation of subject matter are made by people other than the artist. These are obvious examples of the ways in which the work is dependent upon not only the artist but the community. Such examples provide reasons to see the arts as subordinate to other philosophical and political enterprises, and ultimately to deny that they are the proper subject matter of philosophy.

The practice of art is generally acknowledged as creative. To say that it is creative is to imply that in some sense art goes beyond itself into the new. It is part of the essence of art that it have no essence, that is, that there exists no one necessary element or component which binds art together. To insist on the existence of a necessary element or essential features, either of its ontology or as a criterion of its value, is to twist and distort the history and practice. If we look for what is *common*, we end up with general and empty criteria, or we end up defining art in such a way that most art is not art. Because art seems to demand this openness, it has always been problematic for the philosopher who is traditionally looking for closure, for essences, for necessary and sufficient conditions. We have already considered some philosophers' response to the fact that these features are not to be found in art. They have denigrated or distorted it by putting it into a framework which ill becomes it.

In the history of art we can see these changes taking place. A style becomes popular. Perhaps it is started by an artist, or by popular interest in another type of art (Chinese art has influenced Western art from time to time), or because of the patronage of a person or organization which wants to promote an idea (Nazi art or Counter-Reformation art). The reason can be any one of these, all of them, or a variety of them. The style might last for a while, as artists influence each other and are in turn influenced. This can happen until, for any variety of reasons, the style is played out. It no longer captures the imagination of the public or the artist or the academics. Any number of examples from the history of art could be found to follow such a progression. To take a well-known example, the stylistic shift from French Academic painting to Impressionism shows a dramatic change in aesthetic values. It also is an example of a shift in authority, since the Impressionist painters achieved their popularity outside of the academy and consequently were able to force concessions from that body.

The reasons for a style or an individual's work rising and falling are not fixed. This is why the representation of stylistic change given above is so sketchy. It is necessary to avoid the impression that any one set of factors will necessarily prevail. At different times the same or different influences will have different effects. No formula is known for change or success. In fact, not only do styles change, but they do so retroactively. Other eras find the work of a time interesting or uninteresting. Fashions of aesthetic evaluation evolve. This whole picture of changes in evaluation is one to which Nietzsche is sympathetic.

When we have a stylistic shift, we find that the tools of evaluation which were appropriate to the earlier type of art are often entirely inappropriate to judging the new. This is easy to see in a case as radical as that of the change from the style of the French Academy to Impressionism. Judged by the previous standards, the new art is merely a bad piece of art. The Impressionist art does not have a lofty subject matter. Its treatment is not dramatic. Its linear development is not precise. In order to see this art as valuable or good (let alone to create it), even the critics must go beyond what they "know."

If artists are really continually generating something new, then what they create will often not fit into the values (criteria) which have grown up around a previous type of art. They have "grown up" because the values are not found: they are created just as the art is created.

When, by following Nietzsche, we consider art from the spectator's point of view, we can see how the perspective on art changes from that which focuses on the activity, from its creative aspect, to the perspective of the viewer where the art is now a product and an artifact. Hence, the authority shifts from the artist to the spectator, observer, critic, and judge. Nietzsche is not happy with the shift because it fits in with the kind of perspective he has been criticizing. He thinks that we have favored this viewpoint for many bad reasons. It tends to not acknowledge change, and is therefore conservative. The perspective makes it seem as if values cannot change. This is a retardant to innovation. It has contained an anti-sensual bias because it defines itself as being outside of both history and the realm of sensibility. When this shift in authority (to the spectator) happens, we can focus on criteria of evaluation and try to build a framework for evaluation outside of the work itself. We can try to fit it into what we already have: a canon of art, a style within an academy or culture.

In this sense, we look at art, not as being new, but as something judged in relation to a standard which may not be able to accommodate it. The fact that it is judged in relation to other things is not in itself bad. On the contrary, this acknowledges that art gets its meaning in relation to the cultural context. What is bad is when we do not allow art to take us outside of that realm. We close ourselves off from the most powerful effects of it. We ignore the sensual elements (the de-emphasis of the sensual is not the only issue here, but it is one which emerges as central in a Christian and Puritanical culture and philosophy) for the sake of elements which do not threaten us, do not demand much from us. Thus, the perspective of the spectator functions as the perspective of the God, the omnipotent judge, once did. This perspective protects us from what does not fit into our community of values. It allows us to ignore what we fear and what threatens our "control" of the world.

What, then, is an example of a good judge in the context of aesthetic evaluation, one who is not a slave of communal, which is to say past, values? Critics, if they are to have any place at all, must be willing to be flexible, to be open to new possibilities. Nietzsche would find the following assessment of Leo Steinberg by Jasper Johns a high compliment paid to that critic. Johns writes:

> ... [it] seemed to me that he tried to deal directly with the work and not put his own map of preconceptions over it. He saw the work as something new, and then tried to change himself in relation to it, which is very hard to do. I admired him for that.[8]

Steinberg's work was, at least when it first came out, something to tax the powers of contemporary critics. He often used contemporary, even pop subject matter and traditional materials, or the reverse. But, for our purposes the real point here is that Steinberg seemed to Johns to have an understanding of art which allowed him to create a "system" of evaluation which rested on a new way of seeing, feeling, or being. It is not a system at all. It is a relation or attitude which allowed the critic to change in response to the work. What we do not see here is that attempt to control which Nietzsche believes is motivated by fear. Instead, the values grew up around the work. This is better than asking that the work conform to the value.

This is the model of the critic, and of the philosopher, which Nietzsche wants us to consider, that is, a person who will respond to what is new and what is different: one who both dares to create outside of a canon, and to evaluate outside of the accepted communal values. As we have seen, the bad critic is one who judges from outside. Perhaps Nietzsche is even more radical. Could he mean that the bad critic is one who judges at all? This is true if one considers the distinction between passing judgment and evaluation. The world is full of evaluation which is necessary to us. But a style of sitting in judgment is the main object of Nietzsche's critique. This was considered when discussing his views of moral judgment. In this sense, philosophy is not trying to bind and control life, but to be open to its possibilities and to create possibilities beyond what we have seen. The point is to open people up to new possibilities, not to let their framework prevent them from seeing the possibilities.

In looking at art, we should consider it from the point of view of its creator or creation. "Creation" emphasizes the cultural nature of its coming into being. When we look at art from the artist's point of view, from the most involved perspective, we see that the activity of the artist is a kind of projection. But what kind of projection? Again, not one aimed at taking possession, making concrete or conceptual.

> Great Dilemma: is philosophy an art or a science? Both in its purposes and its results it is an art. But it uses the same means as science—conceptual representation. Philosophy is a form of artistic invention. There is no appropriate category for philosophy; consequently, we must make up and characterize a species (for it) ....
> *The natural history of the philosopher*. He knows in that he invents, and he invents in that he knows.
> He does not grow: I mean, philosophy does not follow the course of the other sciences, even if certain of the philosopher's territories gradually fall into the hands of science. Heraclitus can never be obsolete. Philosophy is invention beyond the limits of experience; it is the continuation of the *mythical drive*. It is thus essentially pictorial. Mathematical expression is not a part of the essence of philosophy.
> Overcoming of knowledge by means of the powers that *fashion myths*.[9]

An openness is necessary for the exercise of the mythic drive, which implies, as we have seen, that art cannot have an essence. Art is in time and history, but it goes beyond itself. It is in a culture, but its meaning may well extend the notion of meaningfulness within that culture. Its influence may extend it beyond that meaning which the artist gives it, to single or multiple meanings which the critic and culture give it. The critic is not supposed to make the work dead or harmless, but to see what it demands of him or her, or us, and what we can get out of it. The good critics let the art take them along to a new world or way of seeing.

In order to do this, some criticism of the existing aesthetic or moral standards will be necessary. These will not necessarily involve long commentary or extended refutation. Criticism is implied in the turning away from some former value. "One refutes a matter by laying it respectfully on ice—"[10] To ignore something is sometimes the most powerful and effective refutation.

As we have noted from the previous chapters, one of the results of the examination of Western philosophy and metaphysics was the discovery that it was based upon beliefs which we can no longer endorse. Nietzsche had offered a:

> *Critique of the concept "true and apparent world."*—Of these, the first is a mere fiction, constructed of fictitious entities. "Appearance" itself belongs to reality: it is a form of its being; i.e., in a world where there is no being, a certain calculable world of identical cases must first be created through appearance: ... the world, apart from our condition of living in it, the world that we have not reduced to our being, our logic and psychological prejudices, does not exist as a world "in-itself"; it is essentially a world of relationships; under certain conditions it has a differing aspect from every point ....[11]

As we can see, this skepticism about the possibility of metaphysics, (or of answering any questions about "being as such") had consequences for epistemology. It certainly has consequences for any notion of truth which fits a correspondence model. That to which our truth or idea would correspond is precisely what we cannot know. Our notion of reality must be tied to knowing. Notions of being and reality must be relational—tied to the knowers themselves. What has been called Nietzsche's perspectivism is the particular way in which Nietzsche deals with this issue. As I have shown in Chapter One, Nietzsche's critique of Platonic and Christian metaphysics includes Kant and positivism. This is so, precisely because he believes that the pursuit of truth, (where truth is defined as a demand for certainty), is still attached to a view of the world which acknowledges that certainty is possible, a view which sees at least some things in that reality as unchanging. In *Philosophy in the Tragic Age of the Greeks*, we see an example of Nietzsche's point, but there the examples were Parmenides representing the metaphysical element, and Heraclitus with his notion of flux, which Nietzsche sees as more akin to his own views.

The perspectives Nietzsche has criticized so far (Platonic, Christian, Kantian) are those which begin by standing outside of the situation. The value under consideration is then extracted from the situation. This value is seen as static, a "calculable world of identical cases." Nietzsche has criticized these perspectives in the context of a variety of philosophical perspectives: ontological, epistemological, and metaphysical. As we have seen, an enormous amount of philosophy has been annihilated by his critique. Now we look at what he has to recommend. It is this which will replace the enormous number of approaches he has discredited.

In artistic activity, particularly the creations of the artist, Nietzsche finds a potent metaphor for a way of knowing which is responsive, takes into consideration change, and has the power to transform our realities. Instead of being interested in control, it helps us to expand ourselves and our sense of the world. This is represented in the case of music:

> *One must learn to love.*—This is what happens to us in music: First one has to *learn to hear* a figure and melody at all, to detect and distinguish it, to isolate it and delimit it as a separate life. Then it requires some exertion and good will to *tolerate* it in spite of its strangeness, to be patient with its appearance and expression, and kindhearted about its oddity. Finally there comes a moment when we are *used* to it, when we wait for it, when we sense that we should miss it if it were missing; and now it continues to compel and enchant us relentlessly until we have become its humble and enraptured lovers who desire nothing better from the world than it and only it.[12]

I began Chapter Four with this quotation about music. In it Nietzsche describes the process by which a person might come to hear a piece of music—hear it and love it. He describes this as an interaction over time. This process requires changes on the part of the person, changes in themselves. The first experience of something new is one of alienation and strangeness. First one has to identify it, see it as separate and different, in order to recognize the sense in the phrase and figure. This sense is not our own sense. It is a new sense interior to the piece. Then we begin to appreciate it—to look for it. This is how we come to learn to know, and to "love," a piece of music.

This passage gives us a good metaphor for what Nietzsche wants from us in both knowing and evaluation. In both cases there must be an openness or receptivity to what is known or under evaluation and consideration. We must take the time to let it affect us—recognizing that it will take time. Knowing and valuing are not formulaic, not a matter of fitting something into a paradigm. Rather they involve us in a process, one which involves challenging the knower to change in relation to the known.

In the first chapter of this work, we saw that Nietzsche rejects a great many standard philosophical methods. He does this on the basis of critical assessments of these methods. In Chapter One, we were less interested in the accuracy of his historical critiques than in finding out what Nietzsche believed was left after them. As a consequence, we passed over a great deal of controversial material in order to get to what Nietzsche believed were some of the possibilities left for philosophy, *if* his criticisms were correct. Nietzsche's dealings with the history of philosophy and his treatment of various philosophers have received a great deal of justified evaluative attention. But it should be noted that our purpose in rehearsing the historical critiques was to find the reason Nietzsche begins his search for his own philosophy where he does.

This work is called the reclamation of philosophy because I consider Nietzsche to be engaged in a task of reappropriating certain characteristics of past philosophies into his work. For example, he reclaims philosophical reflection as practiced by French moralists (Montaigne, Charron, La Rochefoucauld, Chamfort, Stendhal), some pre-Socratic philosophers (Heraclitus), and German thinkers (Goethe, Heine). Nietzsche acknowledges his ties to these earlier philosophers whose influence he rightly saw to be diminishing.

But he was also interested in reclaiming an attitude which was very much a part of these views, and something which Nietzsche seemed to value very much personally. This attitude was opposed to the dogmatic and transcendental trends Nietzsche found prevalent in most of the philosophy of his day. It was the attempt, achieved by method and style, to infuse vitality, life, and joy into the tasks of morality, artistic creation, and knowing. In our culture, the only remnant we have retained is that found in artistic creation. In other areas, dogmatism has carried the day. It is crucial to note that Nietzsche sees the vestiges of dogmatism in two of the modern world's most important critiques of dogmatism: Kant's critiques and positivism with its demand for certainty.

Another aspect of the philosophy Nietzsche wanted to reclaim or re-create was one which acknowledged cultural and historical change. This is one of the accomplishments which his genealogies were meant to achieve. We have looked at three of them rather carefully. Nietzsche's genealogies are interesting as examples of one type of philosophical methodology still available to us if we accept (as I do, provisionally, for the purposes of this exploration) Nietzsche's critique of the methods of certain philosophers. It is interesting that his major works on moral and aesthetic value take on this form. We have looked at Nietzsche's exploration of values which arose in a historical, cultural context. His notion of values and value changes are best understood in this context; a close relation exists between the ways in which we are to understand both aesthetic and ethical value. We have seen the cultural reasons why it might be easier for us to accept his notion of a historical context for value change in aesthetics rather than in ethics.

In the previous three chapters, I have considered what Nietzsche has to say about value; particularly what he has to say about moral value. By looking at his views of aesthetic value, we saw his model for moral change. We note, in particular, that this includes his analysis of moral change or revolution. As a mature writer, he is no longer interested in philosophy as merely displaying skill in analytic or logical reasoning. He is interested in a philosophy which can address, in a variety of ways, the cultural and personal issues of people constructing themselves in their world. He is particularly interested in developing and using philosophical talents which help one to see the values implicit in the practices and assumptions people hold. These values are not just moral; they are also epistemologically relevant. The beliefs we have about the world ground our perspectives and allow our knowing.

Nietzsche was a thinker of great breadth. He was interested in issues which arise from our lives as cultural beings, as well as issues which arise within disciplines. We have seen an example of this in his attitude toward philology and the state of the profession as he found it. In his relation to that profession we see his love of language, scholarship, and yet his refusal to be ruled by the stultifying conventions of the discipline. Nietzsche wrote poetry for most of his life. He composed music. The craft of language and the power of style were things which intrigued him and which pushed him to experiment in his own prose. In order to get a sense of Nietzsche the thinker, we must acknowledge the breadth of the work. Yet, in all of his enterprises the embellishment, the intensifying, deepening of our experience of life was his goal. The experience of living is the site where the issues he raises come together. Nietzsche demands that philosophy and all thought serve life. Understanding this is crucial to knowing this multifaceted thinker.

NOTES

Introduction

1. Friedrich Nietzsche, *The Genealogy of Morals*, trans. Francis Golffing (New York: Doubleday & Company, 1956), Preface, §I, p. 149.
2. Cornel West, "Nietzsche's Prefiguration of Postmodern American Philosophy," *Why Nietzsche Now?* (Bloomington: Indiana University Press, 1985).
3. Martin Heidegger, *Nietzsche*, 4 vols., trans. David Farrell Krell, Joan Stambaugh, and Frank A. Capuzzi (San Francisco: Harper and Row, 1979-1982).
4. Friedrich Nietzsche, *The Portable Nietzsche: The Antichrist*, trans. Walter Kaufmann (New York: Viking Press, 1972).
5. Nietzsche, *The Genealogy of Morals*, trans. Golffing, 3rd Essay, §VII, pp. 255-256.
6. Friedrich Nietzsche, *The Gay Science*, trans. Walter Kaufmann (New York: Random House, 1974), §299.
7. Mary Agnes Hamilton, "Nietzsche: The Laughing Philosopher," *Socialist Review* (January 1920), p. 35.
8. Brendan Donnellan, *Nietzsche and the French Moralists* (Bonn: Bouvier, 1982), p. 167.
9. Nietzsche, *The Genealogy of Morals*, trans. Golffing, Preface, §VIII, p. 157.
10. Friedrich Nietzsche, *Philosophy and Truth*, trans. Daniel Breazeale (Atlantic Heights, N.J.: Humanities Press, 1979), *The Philosopher*, §91.
11. Crane Brinton, *Nietzsche* (Cambridge, Mass.: Harvard University Press, 1941), p. vii.
12. *Ibid*., p. 233.
13. *Ibid*., p. 75.
14. *Ibid*., p. xvii.
15. Friedrich Nietzsche, *Human, All Too Human*, vol. 2, Part Two, *The Wanderer and His Shadow*, trans. R. J. Hollingdale (Cambridge, England: Cambridge University Press, 1986), §333.
16. Brinton, *Nietzsche*, p. 235.
17. Hamilton, "Nietzsche: The Laughing Philosopher," p. 35.
18. Nietzsche, *The Gay Science*, Preface, §3, pp. 35, 36.
19. Friedrich Nietzsche, The *Portable Nietzsche*, trans. Walter Kaufmann (New York: Random House, 1974), p. 12.
20. *Ibid*., p. 15.
21. See Nietzsche's notes from the 1870s about method in Nietzsche, *Philosophy and Truth*, trans. Breazeale, *The Philosopher*, §37.
22. Arthur C. Danto, *Nietzsche as Philosopher* (New York: Macmillan Company, 1967), p. 37.
23. Maurice Merleau-Ponty, "Eye and Mind," *The Primacy of Perception*, trans. James M. Edie (Evanston, Ill: Northwestern University Press, 1964), p. 160.
24. Nietzsche, *The Gay Science*, §329.
25. *Ibid*., §7.
26. Michel Foucault, "Nietzsche, Genealogy, History," *Language, Counter-Memory, Practice*, trans. Donald F. Bouchard and Sherry Simmons (Ithaca, N.Y.: Cornell University Press, 1980), pp. 139-164.
27. Cornel West, "The Genealogy of Racism: On the Underside of Modern Discourse," *The Journal: A Journal of Black Culture*, 1:1 (1984), pp. 42-60.

28. *Ibid.*, p. 44.
29. *Ibid.*, p. 43.
30. Kathryn Pyne Parsons (Addelson), "Nietzsche and Moral Change," *Nietzsche*, ed. Robert Solomon (Garden City, N.Y.: Anchor Books, 1973), p. 169.
31. *Ibid.*, pp. 169-170.
32. See for example, Edith Ellis (Lees), *Three Modern Seers* (London: S. Paul, 1910); Georg Simmel, *Schopenhauer and Nietzsche*, trans. Helmut Loiskandl, Deena Weinstein, and Michael Weinstein (Amherst, Mass.: University of Massachusetts, 1986); for a general discussion see also David S. Thatcher, *Nietzsche in England* (Toronto: University of Toronto, 1970); R. Hinton Thomas, *Nietzsche in German Politics and Society, 1890-1918* (Manchester: Manchester University Press, 1986).
33. Hamilton, "Nietzsche: The Laughing Philosopher," pp. 33-34.
34. *Ibid.*, p. 34.
35. Nietzsche, *The Gay Science*, Preface §3, pp. 35, 36.
36. Søren Kierkegaard, *Concluding Unscientific Postscript*, trans. D.F. Swenson and W. Lowrie (Princeton: Princeton University Press, 1944), p. 111.
37. Nietzsche, *The Genealogy of Morals*, trans. Golffing, Preface, §I, p. 149.

Chapter One

1. Friedrich Nietzsche, *Ecce Homo*, trans. Walter Kaufmann (New York: Random House, 1969), "Birth of Tragedy," §3, p. 273.
2. Friedrich Nietzsche, *The Will to Power*, trans. Walter Kaufmann and R. J. Hollingdale (New York: Random House, 1967), §275 (1883-1888).
3. Friedrich Nietzsche, *On the Genealogy of Morals*, trans. Walter Kaufmann (New York: Random House, 1969), 1st Essay, §15.
4. *Ibid.*
5. Nietzsche, *The Will to Power*, §588.
6. Nietzsche, *On the Genealogy of Morals*, trans. Kaufmann, 3rd Essay, §24.
7. Friedrich Nietzsche, *Daybreak*, trans. R. J. Hollingdale (Cambridge, England: Cambridge University Press, 1983), Preface, §4.
8. Friedrich Nietzsche, *The Gay Science*, trans. Walter Kaufmann (New York: Random House, 1974), §108.
9. *Ibid.*, §125.
10. Nietzsche, *Daybreak*, §149.
11. Nietzsche, *Ecce Homo*, "Why I Am a Destiny," §8, p. 334.
12. Nietzsche, *The Gay Science*, §341.
13. Cf. the wisdom of Silenus, Friedrich Nietzsche, *The Birth of Tragedy*, trans. Francis Golffing (New York: Doubleday & Company, 1956), §3, p. 29.
14. Friedrich Nietzsche, *Philosophy and Truth*, trans. Daniel Breazeale (Atlantic Heights, N.J.: Humanities Press, 1979), *The Philosopher*, §37.
15. Nietzsche, *Ecce Homo*, "Birth of Tragedy," §3.
16. Nietzsche, *Beyond Good and Evil*, trans. Walter Kaufmann (New York: Random House, 1966), §10 and §204, and *The Will to Power*, trans. Walter Kaufmann and R. J. Hollingdale (New York: Random House, 1967), §120.
17. Friedrich Wilhelm Nietzsche, *Philosophy in the Tragic Age of the Greeks*, trans. Marianne Cowan (Chicago: Henry Regnery Company, 1971), p. 31.
18. *Ibid.*, p. 33.
19. Nietzsche, *Philosophy and Truth*, *The Philosopher*, §47.
20. Nietzsche, *The Gay Science*, §347.

21. Nietzsche, *The Will to Power*, §1.
22. Nietzsche, *The Gay Science*, §344.
23. Friedrich Nietzsche, *The Portable Nietzsche: The Antichrist*, trans. Walter Kaufmann (New York: Viking Press, 1972), §47*f*.
24. Nietzsche, *The Will to Power*, §530.
25. Nietzsche, *Daybreak*, Preface, §3.
26. Nietzsche, *The Gay Science*, §109.
27. *Ibid.*
28. Nietzsche, *The Gay Science*, §347, and *The Will to Power*, §1.
29. Nietzsche, *Philosophy in the Tragic Age of the Greeks*, pp. 41-42.
30. *Ibid.*, p. 41.
31. *Ibid.*, pp. 52-53.
32. Nietzsche, *Ecce Homo*, "Birth of Tragedy," §3.
33. Nietzsche, *Philosophy in the Tragic Age of the Greeks*, p. 68.
34. *Ibid.*, p. 81.
35. *Ibid.*, pp. 81-82.
36. *Ibid.*, p. 84.
37. Friedrich Nietzsche, *The Portable Nietzsche: Twilight of the Idols*, trans. Walter Kaufmann (New York: Viking Press, 1972), III, §1.
38. *Ibid.*, p. 479.
39. *Ibid.*, "How the 'True World' Finally Became a Fable," §3, p. 485.
40. Friedrich Nietzsche, *Untimely Meditations: On the Uses and Disadvantages of History for Life*, trans. R. J. Hollingdale (Cambridge, England: Cambridge University Press, 1983), p. 59.
41. Nietzsche, *Philosophy in the Tragic Age of the Greeks*, pp. 5-6; and Nietzsche, *Philosophy and Truth*, trans. Breazeale, *The Philosopher*, §47.
42. Nietzsche, *Philosophy in the Tragic Age of the Greeks*, p. 83.
43. Nietzsche, *Ecce Homo*, "Why I Am a Destiny," §7.
44. Jacques Derrida, *Spurs: Nietzsche's Styles*, trans. Barbara Harlow (Chicago: University of Chicago Press, 1979), p. 81.
45. Nietzsche, *The Portable Nietzsche: Twilight of the Idols*, p. 484.
46. Nietzsche, *Ecce Homo*, "Birth of Tragedy," p. 272.
47. Nietzsche, *The Gay Science*, §343.
48. Nietzsche, *On the Genealogy of Morals*, trans. Kaufmann, 3rd Essay, §7.
49. Nietzsche, *Ecce Homo*, pp. 267-268.
50. Nietzsche, *The Will to Power*, §503.
51. Nietzsche, *Philosophy and Truth*, *The Philosopher*, §43.
52. Nietzsche, *The Will to Power*, §512.
53. Friedrich Nietzsche, *Human, All Too Human*, trans. R. J. Hollingdale (Cambridge, England: Cambridge University Press, 1986), §19.
54. Nietzsche, *Ecce Homo*, "Birth of Tragedy," §3.
55. Nietzsche, *Philosophy and Truth*, *The Philosopher*, §37.

Chapter Two

1. Friedrich Nietzsche, *Human, All Too Human*, trans. R. J. Hollingdale (Cambridge, England: Cambridge University Press, 1986), §25.
2. Friedrich Nietzsche, *The Gay Science*, trans. Walter Kaufmann (New York: Random House, 1974), §343.
3. Nietzsche, *Human, All Too Human*, vol. 2, Part One, *Assorted Opinions and*

Maxims, §17.

4. Nietzsche, *The Gay Science*, §7.

5. *Ibid.*, §382.

6. Friedrich Nietzsche, *The Will to Power*, trans. Walter Kaufmann and R. J. Hollingdale (New York: Random House, 1967), §407.

7. *Ibid.*, §407.

8. *Ibid.*, §408.

9. Friedrich Nietzsche, *Beyond Good and Evil*, trans. Walter Kaufmann (New York: Random House, 1966), §260, p. 205.

10. Nietzsche, *The Gay Science*, §335.

11. Nietzsche, *Beyond Good and Evil*, §187.

12. Nietzsche, *The Gay Science*, §345.

13. Nietzsche, *Beyond Good and Evil*, §187.

14. Nietzsche, *The Gay Science*, §335.

15. Nietzsche, *The Will to Power*, §841.

16. Friedrich Nietzsche, *On the Genealogy of Morals*, trans. Walter Kaufmann (New York: Doubleday & Company, 1956), Preface, §4.

17. Nietzsche, *The Will to Power*, §30.

18. Nietzsche, *The Gay Science*, §345.

19. Nietzsche, *The Will to Power*, §680 (1883-1888).

20. Friedrich Nietzsche, *The Portable Nietzsche: Twilight of the Idols*, trans. Walter Kaufmann (New York: Viking Press, 1972), §12.

21. Nietzsche, *The Gay Science*, §345, p. 284.

22. Nietzsche, *The Genealogy of Morals*, trans. Golffing, Preface, §VI, p. 155.

23. *Ibid.*, Preface III, p. 151.

24. Friedrich Nietzsche, *The Birth of Tragedy*, and *The Case of Wagner*, trans. Walter Kaufmann (New York: Vintage Books, 1967), Epilogue, p. 190.

25. Nietzsche, *The Genealogy of Morals*, trans. Golffing, Preface, §V, p. 153.

26. Nietzsche, *The Gay Science*, §345.

27. *Ibid.*

28. Friedrich Wilhelm Nietzsche, *Werke*, vol. 3, Herausgegeben von Karl Schlechta (Frankfurt/M: Verlag Ullstein GmbH, 1979), *Jenseits von Gut und Böse*, II, p. 730; *Der Fall Wagner*, Epilog II, p. 937.

29. Nietzsche, *The Birth of Tragedy*, and *The Case of Wagner*, p. 190.

30. Nietzsche, *Beyond Good and Evil*, §287.

31. *Ibid.*, §282.

32. Alexander Nehamas, *Nietzsche: Life as Literature* (Cambridge, Mass.: Harvard University Press, 1985).

33. Nietzsche, *The Genealogy of Morals*, trans. Golffing, 1st Essay, §II, p. 160.

34. Nietzsche, *Werke*, vol. 3, Herausgegeben von Karl Schlechta, *Jenseits von Gut und Böse*, II, p. 730.

35. Nietzsche, *Beyond Good and Evil*, §260, p. 207.

36. George Eliot, *The Mill on the Floss* (New York: Thomas Nelson and Sons, 1925), p. 394.

37. Nietzsche, *The Genealogy of Morals*, trans. Golffing, 1st Essay, §X, p. 172.

38. Emma Goldman, *Living My Life* (Salt Lake City, Utah: Peregrine Smith Books, 1982), p. 194.

39. Nietzsche, *The Genealogy of Morals*, trans. Golffing, 1st Essay, §X, p.

170.

40. Nietzsche, *The Birth of Tragedy*, and *The Case of Wagner*, Epilogue, p. 190.

41. Friedrich Nietzsche, *The Portable Nietzsche: Thus Spoke Zarathustra*, trans. Walter Kaufmann (New York: Viking Press, 1972), "On Higher Men," p. 400.

42. Nietzsche, *The Birth of Tragedy*, and *The Case of Wagner*, pp. 191-192.

43. Nietzsche, *The Genealogy of Morals*, trans. Golffing, 3rd Essay, p. 261.

44. Nietzsche, *The Gay Science*, §335.

45. Nietzsche, *The Portable Nietzsche: The Antichrist*, p. 638.

46. Nietzsche, *The Genealogy of Morals*, trans. Golffing, 1st Essay, §XI, p. 174.

47. Nietzsche, *Human, All Too Human*, §25.

48. Nietzsche, *The Gay Science*, §335.

49. *Ibid.*

50. Simone de Beauvoir, *Memoirs of a Dutiful Daughter*, trans. James Kirkup (Cleveland: World Publishing Company, 1959), p. 340.

Chapter Three

1. Friedrich Nietzsche, *The Gay Science*, trans. Walter Kaufmann (New York: Random House, 1974), §299.

2. Friedrich Nietzsche, *Human, All Too Human*, vol. 2, Part One, *Assorted Opinions and Maxims*, trans. R. J. Hollingdale (Cambridge, England: Cambridge University Press, 1986), §25, §164, §176.

3. Friedrich Nietzsche, *The Will to Power*, trans. Walter Kaufmann and R. J. Hollingdale (New York: Random House, 1967), §811 (1888).

4. This was brought to my attention by John Atwell of Temple University.

5. Friedrich Nietzsche, *Daybreak*, trans. R. J. Hollingdale (Cambridge, England: Cambridge University Press, 1983), §172, for Plato; Nietzsche, *The Will to Power*, §§851-852, for Aristotle; Nietzsche, *Human, All Too Human*, §212.

6. Leo Tolstoy, *What Is Art?*, trans. Aylmer Maude (Oxford: Oxford University Press, 1950).

7. Plato, *Ion, Republic* 10.1-8, and Iris Murdoch, *The Fire and the Sun: Why Plato Banished the Artists* (Oxford: Oxford University Press, 1978).

8. Aristotle, *Poetics*, 1449b, 28*ff*.

9. Nietzsche, *Daybreak*, §448.

10. Nietzsche, *The Gay Science*, §370.

11. Friedrich Nietzsche, *Beyond Good and Evil*, trans. Walter Kaufmann (New York: Random House, 1966), §33.

12. *Ibid.*

13. Nietzsche, *Human, All Too Human*, vol. 2, Part One, *Assorted Opinions and Maxims*, §406.

14. Nietzsche, *The Will to Power*, §811.

15. Friedrich Nietzsche, *The Genealogy of Morals*, trans. Francis Golffing (New York: Doubleday & Company, 1956), 3rd Essay, §VII, p. 241.

16. *Ibid.*, p. 238.

17. *Ibid.*, p. 239.

18. *Ibid.*, p. 238.

19. *Ibid.*

20. Nietzsche, *The Gay Science*, §299.

21. Nietzsche, *Beyond Good and Evil*, §7.

22. Nietzsche, *The Gay Science*, §373.

23. Nietzsche, *Philosophy in the Tragic Age of the Greeks*, trans. Marianne Cowan (Chicago: Henry Regnery Company, 1971), p. 25.

24. Nietzsche, *Beyond Good and Evil*, §11.

25. *Ibid*., §188.

26. *Ibid*., §11.

27. Nietzsche, *The Gay Science*, §351.

28. Nietzsche, *Beyond Good and Evil*, Preface, p. 3.

29. Friedrich Wilhelm Nietzsche, *Ecce Homo*, trans. Walter Kaufmann (New York: Random House, 1969).

30. Nietzsche, *The Will to Power*, §148.

31. Nietzsche, *Beyond Good and Evil*, §75.

32. Nietzsche, *Philosophy in the Tragic Age of the Greeks*, p. 88.

33. *Ibid*., p. 79.

34. *Ibid*., p. 80.

35. *Ibid*., p. 52.

36. *Ibid*., p. 62.

37. Friedrich Nietzsche, *Philosophy and Truth*, trans. Daniel Breazeale (Atlantic Heights, N.J.: Humanities Press, 1979), *The Philosopher*, p. 74.

38. Friedrich Nietzsche, *The Birth of Tragedy*, trans. Francis Golffing (New York: Doubleday & Company, 1956) and *Ecce Homo*.

39. Nietzsche, *The Birth of Tragedy*, trans. Golffing, p. 19.

40. Nietzsche, *Philosophy in the Tragic Age of the Greeks*, p. 2.

41. Friedrich Nietzsche, *The Birth of Tragedy*, and *The Case of Wagner*, trans. Walter Kaufmann (New York: Vintage Books, 1967), p. 42.

42. Nietzsche, *The Birth of Tragedy*, trans. Golffing, pp. 21-22.

43. Nietzsche, *The Birth of Tragedy*, trans. Kaufmann, p. 46.

44. *Ibid*., p. 74.

45. *Ibid*., p. 78.

46. *Ibid*., pp. 83-84.

47. *Ibid*., p. 69.

48. *Ibid*., p. 73.

49. *Ibid*., p. 48.

50. J. H. Groth, "Wilamowitz-Möllendorf on Nietzsche's *Birth of Tragedy*," *Journal of the History of Ideas*, 2 (1950), pp. 179-190.

51. Nietzsche, *Philosophy in the Tragic Age of the Greeks*, pp. 5-6.

52. Friedrich Wilhelm Nietzsche, *The Complete Works of Nietzsche*, trans. Oscar B. Levy and William A. Haussman (New York: Macmillan Company, 1924), Vol. 8, pp. 109-190.

53. Friedrich Nietzsche, *Untimely Meditations: On the Uses and Disadvantages of History for Life*, trans. R. J. Hollingdale (Cambridge, England: Cambridge University Press, 1983), p. 59.

54. Nietzsche, *The Birth of Tragedy*, trans. Golffing, p. 3.

55. Nietzsche, *The Birth of Tragedy*, "Attempt at Self Criticism," see also *Ecce Homo*.

56. Nietzsche, *Philosophy in the Tragic Age of the Greeks*.

57. E. M. Butler, *The Tyranny of Greece over Germany* (Boston: Beacon Hill Press, 1958).

58. Nietzsche, *The Will to Power*, §830.

59. Nietzsche, *Philosophy in the Tragic Age of the Greeks*, p. 1.

60. Nietzsche, *The Birth of Tragedy*, trans. Kaufmann, p. 52.

61. Walter Kaufmann, *Nietzsche: Philosopher, Psychologist, Antichrist* (Cleveland: Meridian, (1961, 1st ed.), p. 123.

62. Nietzsche, *The Birth of Tragedy*, trans. Kaufmann, p. 59.

63. *Ibid.*

64. Friedrich Nietzsche, *The Portable Nietzsche: Twilight of the Idols*, trans. Walter Kaufmann (New York: Viking Press, 1972), p. 473.

65. Nietzsche, *Philosophy in the Tragic Age of the Greeks*, p. 13.

66. Nietzsche, *The Birth of Tragedy*, §18.

67. Nietzsche, *The Portable Nietzsche: Twilight of the Idols*, p. 484.

68. Nietzsche, *The Birth of Tragedy*, trans. Golffing, p. 52.

69. Nietzsche, *Untimely Meditations: On the Uses and Disadvantages of History for Life*, p. 60.

70. Nietzsche, *The Gay Science*, §299.

Chapter Four

1. Friedrich Nietzsche, *The Gay Science*, trans. Walter Kaufmann (New York: Random House, 1974), §334.

2. Friedrich Nietzsche, *The Will to Power*, trans. Walter Kaufmann and R. J. Hollingdale (New York: Random House, 1967), §794.

3. Friedrich Nietzsche, *The Birth of Tragedy*, and *The Case of Wagner*, trans. Walter Kaufmann (New York: Vintage Books, 1967), Preface.

4. Nietzsche, *The Gay Science*, §370.

5. *Ibid.*

6. Friedrich Nietzsche, *The Portable Nietzsche: Nietzsche Contra Wagner*, trans. Walter Kaufmann (New York: Viking Press, 1972), p. 671.

7. Friedrich Nietzsche, *Human, All Too Human*, vol. 2, Part One, *Assorted Opinions and Maxims*, §19. trans. R. J. Hollingdale (Cambridge, England: Cambridge University Press, 1986).

8. Carter Radcliff, "The Inscrutable Jasper Johns: The Anatomy of His Melancholic Brilliance," *Vanity Fair*, 1:1 (February 1984), p. 65.

9. Friedrich Nietzsche, *Philosophy and Truth*, trans. Daniel Breazeale (Atlantic Heights, N.J.: Humanities Press, 1979), *The Philosopher*, §53, p. 19.

10. Friedrich Nietzsche, *The Portable Nietzsche: The Antichrist*, trans. Walter Kaufmann (New York: Viking Press, 1972), p. 637.

11. Nietzsche, *The Will to Power*, §568.

12. Nietzsche, *The Gay Science*, §334.

BIBLIOGRAPHY

Allison, David B., ed. *The New Nietzsche: Contemporary Styles of Interpretation* (New York: Dell Publishers, 1977).

Aristotle. *Nicomachean Ethics*, trans. Terence Irwin (Indianapolis: Hackett Publishing, 1985).

_______. *The Poetics of Aristotle: Translation and Commentary*, trans. Stephen Halliwell (Chapel Hill: University of North Carolina Press, 1987).

Aschheim, Steven E. *The Nietzsche Legacy in Germany: 1890-1990* (Berkeley: University of California, 1992).

Atwell, John. "Nietzsche's Perspectivism," *Southern Journal of Philosophy*, 19 (Summer 1980), pp. 157-170.

_______. "The Significance of Dance in Nietzsche's Thought." Although this paper is published, the references are to an earlier unpublished version.

Babich, Babette E. *Nietzsche's Philosophy of Science: Reflecting Science on the Ground of Art and Life* (Albany: State University of New York, 1994).

Bataille, Georges. *On Nietzsche*, trans. Bruce Boone (New York: Paragon House, 1994).

Beauvoir, Simone de. *Memoirs of a Dutiful Daughter*, trans. James Kirkup (Cleveland: World Publishing Company, 1959).

Brinton, Crane. *Nietzsche* (Cambridge, Mass.: Harvard University Press, 1941).

Burgard, Peter J., ed. *Nietzsche and the Feminine* (Charlottesville: University of Virginia Press, 1994).

Butler, E. M. *The Tyranny of Greece over Germany* (Boston: Beacon Hill Press, 1958).

Campbell, Thomas Moody. "Aspects of Nietzsche's Struggle with Philology to 1871," *The Germanic Review*, 12:4 (October 1937), pp. 251-266.

_______. "Nietzsche and the Academic Mind," *PMLA*, 62, Supplement (1947), pp. 1183-1196.

Clark, Maudemarie. *Nietzsche on Truth and Philosophy* (Cambridge, England: Cambridge University Press, 1990).

Coulter, James A. "Nietzsche and Greek Studies," *Greek, Roman, and Byzantine Studies*, 3:1 (Winter 1960), pp. 46-51.

Danto, Arthur C. *Nietzsche as Philosopher* (New York: Macmillan Company, 1967).

Deleuze, Gilles. *Nietzsche and Philosophy*, trans. Hugh Tomlinson (New York: Columbia University Press, 1983).

Derrida, Jacques. *Spurs: Nietzsche's Styles*, trans. Barbara Harlow (Chicago: University of Chicago Press, 1979).

Donnellan, Brendan. *Nietzsche and the French Moralists* (Bonn: Bouvier, 1982).

Eliot, George. *The Mill on the Floss* (New York: Thomas Nelson and Sons, 1925).

Ellis, Edith M. (Lees). *Three Modern Seers* (London: S. Paul, 1910).

Ellis, Havelock. *Affirmations* (Boston: Longwood Press, 1977).

Foucault, Michel. "Nietzsche, Genealogy, History," *Language, Counter-Memory, Practice*, trans. Donald F. Bouchard and Sherry Simmons (Ithaca, N.Y.: Cornell University Press, 1980).

Gilman, Sander L., ed. *Conversations with Nietzsche: A Life in the Words of His Contemporaries*, trans. David J. Parent (Oxford: Oxford University Press, 1987).

Goldman, Emma. *Living My Life* (Salt Lake City, Utah: Peregrine Smith Books, 1982).

Groth, J. H. "Wilamowitz-Möllendof on Nietzsche's Birth of Tragedy," *Journal of the History of Ideas*, 2 (1950), pp. 179-190.

Hamilton, Mary Agnes. "Nietzsche: The Laughing Philosopher," *Socialist Review* (January 1920).

Hayman, Ronald. *Nietzsche: A Critical Life* (New York: Penguin Books, 1982).

Heidegger, Martin. *Nietzsche*, 4 vols., trans. David Farrell Krell, Joan Stambaugh, and Frank A. Capuzzi (San Francisco: Harper and Row, 1979-1982).

Hollingdale, R. J. *Nietzsche* (London: Routledge and Kegan Paul, 1973).

Kant, Immanual. *The Foundations of the Metaphysics of Morals*, trans. Lewis White Beck (New York: Bobbs-Merrill, 1959).

Kaufmann, Walter. *Nietzsche: Philosopher, Psychologist, Antichrist*, 1st ed. (Cleveland: Meridian, 1961).

________. *Nietzsche: Philosopher, Psychologist, Antichrist*, 4th ed. (Princeton: Princeton University Press, 1974).

Kierkegaard, Søren. *Concluding Unscientific Postscript*, trans. D. F. Swenson and W. Lowrie (Princeton: Princeton University Press, 1944).

Kofman, Sarah. *Nietzsche and Metaphor*, trans. Duncan Lange (Stanford, California: Stanford University Press, 1993).

Merleau-Ponty, Maurice. *The Primacy of Perception*, trans. James M. Edie, ed. (Evanston, Ill.: Northwestern University Press, 1964).

Murdoch, Iris. *The Fire and the Sun: Why Plato Banished the Artists* (Oxford: Oxford University Press, 1978).

Nehamas, Alexander. *Nietzsche: Life as Literature* (Cambridge, Mass.: Harvard University Press, 1985).

Nietzsche, Friedrich Wilhelm. *Beyond Good and Evil*, trans. Walter Arnold Kaufmann (New York: Random House, 1966).

_______. *Beyond Good and Evil*, trans. Helen Zimmern (Buffalo: Prometheus Books, 1989).

_______. *The Birth of Tragedy*, and *The Case of Wagner*, trans. Walter Kaufmann (New York: Random House, 1967).

_______. *The Birth of Tragedy* and *The Genealogy of Morals*, trans. Francis Golffing (New York: Doubleday & Company, 1956).

_______. *The Complete Works of Friedrich Nietzsche*, ed. Oscar B. Levy, 18 vols. (London: George Allen & Unwil Ltd., 1924).

_______. *Daybreak*, trans. R. J. Hollingdale (Cambridge, England: Cambridge University Press, 1983).

_______. *Dithyrambs of Dionysus*, trans. R. J. Hollingdale (Redding Ridge, Connecticut: Black Swan Books, 1984).

_______. *The Gay Science*, trans. Walter Kaufmann (New York: Random House, 1974).

_______. *Human, All Too Human*, trans. Marion Faber (Lincoln: University of Nebraska Press, 1984).

_______. *Human, All Too Human*, trans. R. J. Hollingdale (Cambridge, England: Cambridge University Press, 1986).

_______. "Nietzsche's Lecture Notes on Rhetoric: A Translation," trans. Carole Blair, *Philosophy and Rhetoric*, 16:2 (1983), pp. 94-129.

_______. *On the Genealogy of Morals and Ecce Homo*, trans. Walter Kaufmann (New York: Random House, 1969).

_______. *Philosophy and Truth*, trans. Daniel Breazeale (Atlantic Heights, New Jersey: Humanities Press, 1979).

_______. *Philosophy in the Tragic Age of the Greeks*, trans. Marianne Cowan (Chicago: Henry Regnery Company, 1971).

_______. *The Portable Nietzsche: Twilight of the Idols, The Antichrist, Nietzsche Contra Wagner, Thus Spake Zarathustra*, trans. Walter Kaufmann (New York: Viking Press, 1972).

_______. *Selected Letters of Friedrich Nietzsche*, ed. Oscar B. Levy (New York: Doubleday, 1921).

_______. *Untimely Meditations: David Strauss, the Confessor and Writer, On the Uses & Disadvantages of History for Life, Schopenhauer as Educator, Richard Wagner in Bayreuth*, trans. R. J. Hollingdale (Cambridge, England: Cambridge University Press, 1983).

_______. *Werke.* Herausgegeben von Karl Schlechta, 5 vols. (Frankfurt/M: Verlag Ullstein GmbH, 1979).

_______. *The Will to Power*, trans. Walter Kaufmann and R. J. Hollingdale (New York: Random House, 1967).

O'Hara, Daniel T., ed. *Why Nietzsche Now?* (Bloomington: Indiana University Press, 1985).

Plato. *The Collected Dialogues of Plato*, ed. Edith Hamilton, "Ion," trans. Lane Cooper (New York: Pantheon Books, 1961).

_______. *The Republic*, trans. Robin Waterfield (Oxford: Oxford University Press, 1993).

Radcliff, Carter. "The Inscrutable Jasper Johns: The Anatomy of His Melancholic Brilliance," *Vanity Fair*, 1:1 (February 1984), p. 65.

Reginster, Bernard. "*Ressentiment*, Evaluation and Integrity," *International Studies in Philosophy*, 27:3 (1995) pp. 117-124.

Schlechta, Karl. *International Nietzsche Bibliography* (Chapel Hill, N.C.: University of North Carolina Press, 1960).

Schutte, Ofelia. *Beyond Nihilism: Nietzsche Without Masks* (Chicago: University of Chicago Press, 1984).

Simmel, Georg. *Schopenhauer and Nietzsche*, trans. Helmut Loiskandl, Deena Weinstein, and Michael Weinstein (Amherst: University of Massachusetts, 1986).

Solomon, Robert C., ed. *Nietzsche: A Collection of Critical Essays* (Garden City, N.Y.: Doubleday, 1973).

Stöcker, Helene. "Frauengedanken" and "Nietzsche's Frauenfeindschaft," *Die Liebe und die Frauen* (Berlin: 1908).

_______. "Unsere Umwertung der Werte," in the Swarthmore Peace Collection, Swarthmore, Pennsylvania, dated 1897.

Thatcher, David S. *Nietzsche in England, 1890-1914* (Toronto: University of Toronto, 1970).

Thomas, R. Hinton. *Nietzsche in German Politics and Society, 1890-1918* (Manchester: Manchester University Press, 1986).

Tolstoy, Leo. *What Is Art?*, trans. Aylmer Maude (Oxford: Oxford University Press, 1950).

Vaihinger, Hans. *The Philosophy of "As If", a System of the Theoretical, Practical, and Religious Fictions of Mankind*, trans. Charles Kay Ogden (New York: Harcourt Brace, 1924).

West, Cornel. "The Genealogy of Racism: On the Underside of Modern Discourse," *The Journal: A Journal of Black Culture*, 1:1 (1984), pp. 42-60.

Whitman, James. "Nietzsche in the Magisterial Tradition of German Classical Philology," *Journal of the History of Ideas*, 47:3 (July/September 1986), pp. 453-468.

Yovel, Yirmiyahu, ed. *Nietzsche as Affirmative Thinker* (Dordrecht: Martinus Nijhoff Publishers, 1986).

ABOUT THE AUTHOR

Kathleen J. Wininger is Associate Professor of Philosophy and Chair of the Philosophy Department at the University of Southern Maine. She received her Ph.D. in philosophy from Temple University in 1988 where she also did graduate work in the history of art. Joseph Margolis, Monroe Beardsley, John Fisher, and John Atwell were her teachers of aesthetic theory. Her Bachelor of Arts degree in both Philosophy and Art History is from Southern Connecticut State University with additional work in philosophy at Yale University.

Wininger writes and publishes in the areas of late nineteenth- and twentieth-century philosophy. Her works include articles on ethical theory, Friedrich Nietzsche's moral and aesthetic theories, Decolonization, and the ethical implications of European cinematic portrayal of colonized people. She is currently editing a volume of essays called *Philosophy and Sex*, with Robert Baker of Union College. She teaches courses in Aesthetics, Film Theory, World Philosophy, and Women Thinkers in Africa and the Diaspora. In addition to her present appointment, Wininger has taught at Temple University, Union College, Earlham College, and Villanova University in the United States.

A frequent visitor to East Africa, Wininger was a guest Lecturer at the University of Nairobi in the Autumn of 1996. She taught Philosophy and Women's Studies in Kenya in the Autumn of 1987. In 1996 she was a delegate to the Pan-African Symposium: "Problematics of an African Philosophy: Twenty Years After (1976-1996)" in Addis Ababa, Ethiopia.

INDEX

The Value Inquiry Book Series is co-sponsored by:

American Maritain Association
American Society for Value Inquiry
Association for Personalist Studies
Association for Process Philosophy of Education
Center for East European Dialogue and Development, Rochester Institute of
Technology
Centre for Applied Ethics, Hong Kong Baptist University
College of Education and Allied Professions, Bowling Green State University
Concerned Philosophers for Peace
Conference of Philosophical Societies
International Academy of Philosophy of the Principality of Liechtenstein
International Society for Universalism
International Society for Value Inquiry
Natural Law Society
Philosophical Society of Finland
Philosophy Seminar, University of Mainz
R.S. Hartman Institute for Formal and Applied Axiology
Society for Iberian and Latin American Thought
Society for the Philosophic Study of Genocide and the Holocaust
Yves R. Simon Institute

VIBS

The **Value Inquiry Book Series** is co-sponsored by:

American Maritain Association
American Society for Value Inquiry
Association for Personalist Studies
Association for Process Philosophy of Education
Center for East European Dialogue and Development, Rochester Institute of Technology
Centre for Cultural Research, Aarhus University
College of Education and Allied Professions, Bowling Green State University
Concerned Philosophers for Peace
Conference of Philosophical Societies
International Academy of Philosophy of the Principality of Liechtenstein
International Society for Universalism
International Society for Value Inquiry
Natural Law Society
Philosophical Society of Finland
Philosophy Seminar, University of Mainz
R.S. Hartman Institute for Formal and Applied Axiology
Society for Iberian and Latin-American Thought
Society for the Philosophic Study of Genocide and the Holocaust
Yves R. Simon Institute.

Titles Published

1. Noel Balzer, *The Human Being as a Logical Thinker.*

2. Archie J. Bahm, *Axiology: The Science of Values.*

3. H. P. P. (Hennie) Lötter, *Justice for an Unjust Society.*

4. H. G. Callaway, *Context for Meaning and Analysis: A Critical Study in the Philosophy of Language.*

5. Benjamin S. Llamzon, *A Humane Case for Moral Intuition.*

6. James R. Watson, *Between Auschwitz and Tradition: Postmodern Reflections on the Task of Thinking.* A volume in **Holocaust and Genocide Studies.**

7. Robert S. Hartman, *Freedom to Live: The Robert Hartman Story,* edited by Arthur R. Ellis. A volume in **Hartman Institute Axiology Studies.**

8. Archie J. Bahm, *Ethics: The Science of Oughtness.*

9. George David Miller, *An Idiosyncratic Ethics; Or, the Lauramachean Ethics.*

10. Joseph P. DeMarco, *A Coherence Theory in Ethics.*

11. Frank G. Forrest, *Valuemetrics: The Science of Personal and Professional Ethics.* A volume in **Hartman Institute Axiology Studies.**

12. William Gerber, *The Meaning of Life: Insights of the World's Great Thinkers.*

13. Richard T. Hull, Editor, *A Quarter Century of Value Inquiry: Presidential Addresses of the American Society for Value Inquiry.* A volume in **Histories and Addresses of Philosophical Societies.**

14. William Gerber, *Nuggets of Wisdom from Great Jewish Thinkers: From Biblical Times to the Present.*

15. Sidney Axinn, *The Logic of Hope: Extensions of Kant's View of Religion.*

16. Messay Kebede, *Meaning and Development.*

17. Amihud Gilead, *The Platonic Odyssey: A Philosophical-Literary Inquiry into the* Phaedo.

18. Necip Fikri Alican, *Mill's Principle of Utility: A Defense of John Stuart Mill's Notorious Proof.* A volume in **Universal Justice.**

19. Michael H. Mitias, Editor, *Philosophy and Architecture.*

20. Roger T. Simonds, *Rational Individualism: The Perennial Philosophy of Legal Interpretation.* A volume in **Natural Law Studies.**

21. William Pencak, *The Conflict of Law and Justice in the Icelandic Sagas.*

22. Samuel M. Natale and Brian M. Rothschild, Editors, *Values, Work, Education: The Meanings of Work.*

23. N. Georgopoulos and Michael Heim, Editors, *Being Human in the Ultimate: Studies in the Thought of John M. Anderson.*

24. Robert Wesson and Patricia A. Williams, Editors, *Evolution and Human Values.*

25. Wim J. van der Steen, *Facts, Values, and Methodology: A New Approach to Ethics.*

26. Avi Sagi and Daniel Statman, *Religion and Morality.*

27. Albert William Levi, *The High Road of Humanity: The Seven Ethical Ages of Western Man,* edited by Donald Phillip Verene and Molly Black Verene.

28. Samuel M. Natale and Brian M. Rothschild, Editors, *Work Values: Education, Organization, and Religious Concerns.*

29. Laurence F. Bove and Laura Duhan Kaplan, Editors, *From the Eye of the Storm: Regional Conflicts and the Philosophy of Peace.* A volume in **Philosophy of Peace.**

30. Robin Attfield, *Value, Obligation, and Meta-Ethics.*

31. William Gerber, *The Deepest Questions You Can Ask About God: As Answered by the World's Great Thinkers.*

32. Daniel Statman, *Moral Dilemmas.*

33. Rem B. Edwards, Editor, *Formal Axiology and Its Critics.* A volume in **Hartman Institute Axiology Studies.**

34. George David Miller and Conrad P. Pritscher, *On Education and Values: In Praise of Pariahs and Nomads.* A volume in **Philosophy of Education.**

35. Paul S. Penner, *Altruistic Behavior: An Inquiry into Motivation.*

36. Corbin Fowler, *Morality for Moderns.*

37. Giambattista Vico, *The Art of Rhetoric* (*Institutiones Oratoriae,* 1711-1741), from the definitive Latin text and notes, Italian commentary and introduction by Giuliano Crifò, translated and edited by Giorgio A. Pinton and Arthur W. Shippee. A volume in **Values in Italian Philosophy.**

38. W. H. Werkmeister, *Martin Heidegger on the Way,* edited by Richard T. Hull. A volume in **Werkmeister Studies.**

39. Phillip Stambovsky, *Myth and the Limits of Reason.*

40. Samantha Brennan, Tracy Isaacs, and Michael Milde, Editors, *A Question of Values: New Canadian Perspectives in Ethics and Political Philosophy.*

41. Peter A. Redpath, *Cartesian Nightmare: An Introduction to Transcendental Sophistry.* A volume in **Studies in the History of Western Philosophy.**

42. Clark Butler, *History as the Story of Freedom: Philosophy in Intercultural Context,* with Responses by sixteen scholars.

43. Dennis Rohatyn, *Philosophy History Sophistry.*

44. Leon Shaskolsky Sheleff, *Social Cohesion and Legal Coercion: A Critique of Weber, Durkheim, and Marx.*

45. Alan Soble, Editor, *Sex, Love, and Friendship: Studies of the Society for the Philosophy of Sex and Love, 1977-1992.* A volume in **Histories and Addresses of Philosophical Societies.**

46. Peter A. Redpath, *Wisdom's Odyssey: From Philosophy to Transcendental Sophistry.* A volume in **Studies in the History of Western Philosophy.**

47. Albert A. Anderson, *Universal Justice: A Dialectical Approach.* A volume in **Universal Justice.**

48. Pio Colonnello, *The Philosophy of José Gaos.* Translated from Italian by Peter Cocozzella. Edited by Myra Moss. Introduction by Giovanni Gullace. A volume in **Values in Italian Philosophy.**

49. Laura Duhan Kaplan and Laurence F. Bove, Editors, *Philosophical Perspectives on Power and Domination: Theories and Practices.* A volume in **Philosophy of Peace.**

50. Gregory F. Mellema, *Collective Responsibility.*

51. Josef Seifert, *What Is Life? The Originality, Irreducibility, and Value of Life.* A volume in **Central-European Value Studies.**

52. William Gerber, *Anatomy of What We Value Most.*

53. Armando Molina, *Our Ways: Values and Character,* edited by Rem B. Edwards. A volume in **Hartman Institute Axiology Studies.**

54. Kathleen J. Wininger, *Nietzsche's Reclamation of Philosophy.* A volume in **Central-European Value Studies.**